TABLE OF CONTENTS

PREFACE

Although there is an obvious preference for the movie, "The Spook Who Sat By the Door" in this book's author, there are several other movies selected which, in one way or another, showed an attempted "takeover" of America or, if not that (such as the case of the movie "Triple 9") depict strategy and tactics to expect should such a takeover ever be attempted. These movies are very different but for some reason, each of them shows that America has been targeted by a particular group and that group is organized enough to take down the whole country – or so they thought.

The ten movies to be analyzed in this book are: "The Spook Who Sat By the Door" which deals with a black revolutionary takeover; Invasion of the Body Snatchers" which was originally a 1956 movie that was an actual anti-communism flick using aliens in the place of Russians; two version s of "Red Dawn" where America is attacked with emphasis in the heartland"; a movie called "Badge 373" where Puerto Rican nationalists (in real life they called themselves the Young Lords) in New York City plot and plan to fight against America's imperialistic activities in Puerto Rico, "Invasion USA," which features Chuck Norris defending America against a takeover that originates in Florida and a trilogy of movies called "Rampage," "Rampage: Capital Punishment" and "Rampage: President Down." Finally there is a movie that is more tactical and instructional, "Triple 9," which offers insights on police strategy, tactics and criminal intent – quite revolutionary in the final analysis.

Each of these movies touches upon revolution in their own way. Each has a revolutionary orientation, whether military violence was used or not. In "Invasion of the Body Snatchers" the revolutionary takeover attempt is by aliens and their pods that re-create the images of white people who they kill and then take over their bodies; in "The Spook Who Sat by the Door" it is a race war; in the "Rampage" trilogy its about a young white boy whose goal it is to create worldwide chaos through a series of mass murders; in "Badge 373" a planned revolution is thwarted by racist New York Cop (although all of the planning elements for a revolution are present); in "Invasion USA" America is attacked but the scene is Florida and again, the attempt is thwarted by a lone pro-American cop; and in both "Red Dawn" movies (the latter a modernized re-make), America is attacked with emphasis on the Midwest. The "Rampage Trilogy" is about mass killings and the impact they have on an entire nation, and "Triple 9" is about cops are know the protocols and break them in order to get what they want. Again, quite revolutionary in its content and emphasis.

Movies about revolution and revolutionary activities are serious business for the viewer. Those of us who see America for what it is realize that when the movie is made by white folks and American filmmakers, the white man is always going to win. When the revolution is waged by a white group against other white groups, the group that most closely resembles Euroamerican culture will win.

INTRODUCTION

> "There is no way the United States can police the world and keep us on our ass at the same time without our cooperation …
> "
>
> -- Freeman from, "The Spook Who Sat By The Door"

This fact is lost on the American public, people so caught up in their patriotism and outright racist hatred of the world that they believe that they are literally invincible. So cocky and power-hungry are they that they engage on multiple wars around the world simultaneously, engage in nation-building and propping up leaders that will do their bidding, and act as if they are the world's "police."

Domestically speaking, this has an impact. There are pockets of people all over the nation who are getting fed up. They are beginning to see that the militaristic bullying that this country is exercising on an international level is also being practiced right here at home. The movies that will be reviewed in this book share a common theme: the white man is always right. Even when his intentions are evil or warped, he always comes out on top. His ideas are the best, he is the strongest, he can do whatever he wants and his strategy is always correct. This is what happens on film.

In real life, as we can see here today in 2016, things are not so cut-and-dried. He continues to screw up, over-estimate himself, get duped time and time again, trusts his enemies, and under-estimates people just because he has "vetted" or "screened" or "educated" them. The world's people have a long memory, and those who are waging war on America today are the children of those that America raped, killed, bombed and imposed its will on many years back.

As far as these shores are concerned, this book chose these movies to show how flawed the thinking is. Even when the white man comes out on top, he doesn't learn from past lessons or examples. He doesn't change his ways. He just chalks the suppression of the "revolt" or "uprising" up as "one more win for white nationalism." And this is a mistake that he continues to make even today in ultra-modern America.

"THE SPOOK WHO AT BY THE DOOR": A MOVIE REVIEW

It will become clear to you, after seeing this movie, why it was so difficult to first of all find the book, and why, in recent years, it was so difficult to find the movie. This movie clearly shows white folks what black people could do if we EVER became unified and came to the reality that race relations in America are never going to get better. I call this the STARR – Stelly Theory of American Race Relations. They are as good as they are going to get and these relations are gradually growing worse.

In my view, having control of the cities the way we do, we would whip their ass over time. They would usher in their tanks, machines and guns, and we would engage them in guerilla warfare. In a battle of attrition, they would lose because most of their people, even the brave and bold rifle-totin', tough-talkin' rednecks, would be too spineless to get involved.

Throughout this movie, revolutionary information is provided which provides the perfect formula for doing what needs to be done. Our unity is the white man's biggest fear. That is why he appoints and anoints coons to lead us, uses his media to seduce us with material goods that are sold by nearly-nude white women, and locks our young boys up every chance he gets. But now, with disclaimers at the beginning of the movie by *USA Today* columnist Dewayne Wickham, the movie is being made to appear as some kind of fantasy or a fiction.

That is not the way many black people saw it back in the day. And the movie's serious, sane and well-thought out content shows that Greenlee wasn't kidding around, either. And the Jews who usually green light movies with funding were ignored and Greenlee made the movie on his own. The subject matter plus this lack of financial control by outsiders, are reasons why the movie was feared.

In this book I look at the concept of "uprisings" from a number of vantage points. The chapters include a chapter titled, "Is Revolution Possible? Inevitable?" And then other sections, I offer a letter from revolutionary Assata Shakur and my own views in the "Afterword."

Enjoy – but more importantly, ***learn.***

In my view, the movie breaks down into eight sections: (1) Freeman's initiation into the CIA and that process; (2) Freeman's token 5 year stint at the Agency; (3) Freeman's decision to return to Chicago to accept a social work job, secretly organizing his old gang, the Cobras; (4) Cobra initiation and indoctrination; (5) Pete Dawson enters the picture; (6) the riots trigger the Chicago revolution and national uprising; (6) Freeman exposes him revolutionary bent to

Joy and Dawson; (7) White response to riots is rebuked and (8) the Dawson-Freeman confrontation.

Although these areas are not specifically broken down in this analysis, each of the above represents a turning point in Freeman's revolutionary plan to "get the system off black people's backs." All eight of the above represent political elements which should be discussed as a group, with this analysis being nothing more than a literary fuse that starts the process.

Now, the full analysis begins.

The movie starts out in the office of a white senator who is fighting for his political life in the middle of his re-election campaign. "This is the gun lap for the election," he tells his two advisors, both women, one black and one white. The sister is the more intellectual of the two, apparently oblivious to the fact that she is even black. "The Senator is in solid with the Jews, Mrs. Hennington – the Negroes are the trouble spot," the sister says.

The Senator acts shocked, yelling, "I'm the best friend those people have in Washington." The fact is, following a "law and order" speech he gave, black people got pissed off and pulled away from him. A few points about the movie thus far.

Greenlee hit on several major themes (1) exploitation and concern about the black vote, (2) the priority given to blacks and Jews in elections, despite superior black numbers, (3) the white political belief that one of them could ever be the "best friend" that we could have in Washington and (4) "law and order" speeches and shock by the Senator that black people would receive such a speech positively. Let's explore these points before moving on.

First of all, the concern about and the exploitation of, the black vote. I've seen in action in all the cities I've been in, and the only time I saw it explode in whitey's face was in 1986-87 when I lived in Chicago, and Harold Washington upset racist Jane Byrne. Other than that, in cities like Omaha, the black vote is controlled through Uncle Tom ministers who let these devils come into their churches – mainly the largest church in Omaha, Salem Baptist – and spew forth their lies about what all they are going to do. The same thing takes place in Milwaukee, the 17th largest city in the nation but more politically pitiful than even Omaha, for this reason: Milwaukee has 180,000 black folks and Omaha only has 60,000. And yet the same "this white man is alright wit' me" mentality exists among them.

In Milwaukee, the general population is intellectually bankrupt. In 1991, 90% of high school male seniors from North Division High School had an average grade point average of a D-minus! Their parents, most of them from Mississippi and Alabama, don't know their collective asses from a hole in the ground, either. So the "intelligentsia" in the city takes money in exchange for steering the masses of blacks. Three black newspapers – The Milwaukee Courier, the Milwaukee Community Journal and the Milwaukee Times – have long sold out to the governor, who subsidizes their newspapers so that they can give them away. Trouble is, there are no free lunches so, for the most part, these toms curry favor with whoever is in office. The author of welfare reform Tommy Thompson serve three or four terms and could always rely on these toms to back him. There are two black radio stations in Milwaukee, WNOV and WMCS, and both of them curry favor with the white establishment.

These five institutions alone, combined with the ministers of course, dupe the black masses and direct them politically. That is how racist Mayor John Norquist continued to win the black vote even though he did nothing in the way of jobs. He as brought down when a brave Latina, Marilyn Figueroa, came forward with evidence and documentation that Norquist had blackmailed her for booty, had threatened that if she didn't give him the booty, he would do harm to both blacks and her fellow Latinas. So she stood up for us all, sued him, took him down and he left office in utter embarrassment (but another job, a better job, in Chicago was waiting for him).

I said all that to say all this: Omaha is the 41st largest city and Milwaukee is 17th, *and yet both are manipulated by the kind of black people that Freeman, in the movie, was fighting against.* We therefore have a two-headed enemy: the white man who is trying to kill us all off and the Uncle Tom, who betrays us and carries water for our enemy. Milwaukee has more of both, but Omaha's Toms are more subtle and more willing to mingle with the very people they've sold out. You can also add the coons of Dallas, Texas into this mixture of sellouts, quislings and race-traitors.

This is why the Senator in the movie, could presume that he was "the best friend they've (blacks) have got in Washington, D.C." There are black people who tell these white boys this bullshit. These "negro consultants" who have no credibility in the black community, somehow get the white man to think that they can "deliver" the black vote or that they have "their hands on the pulse of the black community." And because of the low regard these white boys have for us, in general, they retain the services of these toms who, in turn, rock their white master asleep with bullshit about how much he's "loved" in the black community.

Second, the priority given to both blacks and Jews, despite the fact that blacks outnumber Jews ten to one (if not more). Jews have money and clout, and they vote in blocs. They are white first and foremost, but through their money they control black organizations. Those in power want the Jewish vote because Jews have the power of the media behind them. Since Jews control black civil rights organizations, they can "convince" so-called black leadership to "consider" who to vote for. That is why even with our far superior numbers, Jews are given equal and more consideration than black folks are.

In the movie, the Jews were solidly behind the Senator. The blacks split off because of law and order. But remember the time period – the early 1970s when black people were thinking for ourselves. This is when the black-Jewish relationship encountered some difficulties; when black people opened up the history books and saw what Jews had historically done to us, a lot of young blacks got pissed off. These Jews who had exploited us in our communities through "credit," how they controlled civil rights groups, and then later, how they came out against affirmative action and other programs geared toward "leveling the playing field," as they call it.

These Jews think about one thing: Israel. They take their values and beliefs everywhere they go. They come to black meetings, take notes and run back to funding sources and let them know who is saying what about whom. They believe they know black people better than black people know themselves. Racists like Roy Smith, the Mammel Foundation, Bob Wolfson, Lloyd Roitstein and other nickel-slick Jews come off as "liberal," but when it comes to black power, they hate us as much as any gentile cracker. They don't want to hear talk because they know they would be number two (behind the gentile) on the black militant shit list. So they cower, skin and grin, and dupe black people by giving them awards and money so that the black masses will keep thinking that Jews are not white. Remember brothers and sisters: Jews are not a "race." They are a religion, and they are white before they are anything else.

Third, is the belief by the Senator that he could be "the best friend" that black folks have got in Washington, somewhat similar to point number one. But in this case I'm writing about what could be called "The Tarzan Mentality." One point continually driven home by Greenlee in both the book and the movie is the fact that while white folks are willing to concede our athletic superiority, they still think that we are, for the most part, stupid. As a result, it is their "job" to lead us, to show us what to do and how to do it, and so on. This paternalistic racism is what is behind the assumption that they are our "best friend in Washington" despite seeing reams of evidence to the contrary. The lesson here is that white folks lie to themselves and then work hard to make the lie, real.

You see them today: the Kennedys, John Kerrey, Bob Kerrey (who, during the Vietnam War, shot down kids of color and then decided to have a convenient nervous breakdown regretting his actions decades later), or Alan Dershowitz. In Omaha, there's Roy Smith (a liberal by white standards but really a racist in sheep's clothing), Mike Boyle (a fat former mayor who was recalled for calling a black man a "professional nigger" and who now claims to be "good friends" with the very blacks he backstabs) or the current Mayor who thinks putting a jazz statue in North Omaha is an example of "economic development." Milwaukee is no better; former Mayor John Norquist ran on a liberal slate and ended up extorting a Latina for booty, telling her if she didn't give it up, he'd take money away from blacks and Hispanics. And how about the liberals at the University of Wisconsin-Milwaukee, who have thinks like "The Milwaukee Idea" and the "Urban Center," but doesn't see fit to include any blacks folks in their planning?

Fourth, the "law and order speech" and the Senator's naïve belief that black people would respond positively to such a presentation. "Law and order" has always been a code phrase for "black oppression." That is what this movie was all about: dealing with the white man and, true to life, the "revolution" got started in response to what? The police shooting of an unarmed black man. That is what took place in Watts; that is what took place in Newark; that is what took place when cops shot Vivian Strong in Omaha; that is what happened when cops started beating on black people outside of a Detroit bar, The Blind Pig, and black people refused to take it any more. And that Detroit riot, by the way was the worst riot in American history and after it was all over, 43 people were dead and the National Guard was called in. That is what lead to the riots in Milwaukee and the Ernie Lacey and Daniel Bell protests – remember?

"Law and order" – imposed on us by the lawless and the disordered? What kind of bullshit is that? But the theme is what Greenlee was addressing, probably drawing on that "law and order" edict imposed on the country by Richard Nixon (along with some bullshit called "black capitalism") as he won the election in 1972 – a year before the movie came out. More on this later; let's get back to the movie.

The senator needed an idea to 'retrieve the black vote,' as he put it. "Let's see if we can come up with some ideas here," he says to the two women. And they come up with one. The white woman reminds the Senator that the CIA (Central Intelligence Agency) could be accused because of their "racially discriminatory hiring policies." This doesn't really make sense, since the CIA is but one component of an entire governmental system that was not hiring blacks in appropriate numbers. But since the movie is about a CIA-infiltrator, this is how the situation was set up.

At any rate, the woman says, "They have no Negroes except on a menial level." Menial level? A job back then? There was no such thing as a menial government job! It was about the insurance and about taking care of one's family. It wasn't the way it is now where these pecks have to bring in immigrants to do the jobs we won't do. So the concept of a "menial government job" doesn't exactly jibe with the reality of the times in the early 1970s.

The sister and the senator agree with the idea, with the sister stating, "Whomever they select will be the best known spy since 007." How prophetic her words were turn out to be.

According to Carstairs, the white man in charge, there was a recruitment effort and more than two hundred black men were selected. Of hat two hundred, a group of forty was picked and went through trials. Now, as this scene opens, we are in a room where the ten finalists are seated.

The brothers complete what Carstairs calls "our tough preliminary training course," and these are the final ten. Based on their numbers, this prompts this white man to tell them, en are left out of more than 40 that were, "You men, therefore, represent the best of your race." He and his assistant then leave the room.

As soon as the white man leaves the room, they start slapping each other five and acting as if they had already made it. How foolish of them to act and talk this way without even thinking that they are in a CIA building where, logically, every room would be bugged.

They are happy. One brother quips, "We da first spooks to be spooks for the CIA!" Most of them head straight to the bar and the Chivas Regal. Two brothers meet and find out that they belong to the same fraternity. They begin exchanging their silly handshakes. This was a good point because during this interaction, Greenlee is pointing out how shallow and fractionalized black men are. One of those ways is the fraternity system, which of course is present on most college and university campuses.

The fraternity brothers have been duped into thinking that they are something special. They believe that they are doing great things for the community. But behind closed doors, their true nature is revealed, and the issue of competing against other black people and other fraternities shows that they are no better than these outlandishly simplistic black churches who build and expand their physical plant, but offer NOTHING in the way of intellectual development.

As the two fraternity clowns – they claim to be Alphas - exchange their handshakes for example, two other brothers are asking, "Didn't I see you at the Penn Relays, which brings up the fact that most of them got to college because of athletic scholarships. In fact, so did Freeman. But Freeman put his education to work and used it as a basis for increasing his study. The others did what UNO students do: study only when the white man tells you to, read only the pages assigned and do no more than that.

Ironically (or perhaps not) the room they are in is stocked with nothing but a bar filled with alcohol. This is exactly what doomed the Nat Turner rebellion in 1831 – Nat's men wanted to take a break for rest and a drink. Nat initially said no, but the men out voted him. That break cost them and enabled the Militia to catch up with them. Today, when a black man or woman wants to establish a business in the community, these white people will grant a liquor license faster than anything else. In most black communities that you visit, there is a liquor store or lounge on almost every corner. And finally, remember well the role that alcohol – "fire water," as they call it – helped to bring about the defeat of our American Indian brothers and sisters.

At any rate, as the others drink, joke and reminisce, Freeman is in the background, standing and observing. One brother explains the situation they are in:

> It doesn't matter how they feel. The word is integration from the top. Now, some of us have gotta make it, and we're it. You just have to understand the theory of tokenism. They grade on a curve; none of us get too eager, gentlemen, "C" for everybody, right?

This seems to be the philosophy of a number of black people I know (especially the ones on college campuses!), and they all have one thing in common: they are not qualified to do the job they are vying for. They are relying on letters of recommendation, on "knowing" someone inside or on their track records of kissing ass. No intellectual skills whatsoever. In such a situation, like these brothers, you have to rely on the myth of integration and more importantly, that the white man is going to be fair and objective when it comes to selecting you. But just as I tell these sellouts who think they have job security: ***Just because you get picked doesn't mean you're respected,*** and furthermore, "That job is on loan, with the option to Tom."

Again, Freeman is close enough to hear and observe, but not really be seen. Got it?

And all this time, two white men are in another room, watching and listening to everything these black men are talking about. The white men are smiling and laughing. After all, these white men know something that the unsuspecting brothers don't know.

The next several scenes show the intense training that these black men undergo. They learn surveillance, explosive technology, how to sabotage cars, and are taught a key rule in guerilla warfare: "always use the materials that are accessible to any citizen of the country in which you are operating." They learn parachuting, shooting guns and marksmanship, as well as scuba diving. Eventually, the field is whittled down to only six men. The white boys are behind the scenes, convinced and predicting that the athletes will flunk. During his report, one white man says, "Somehow I forgot Freeman even existed. ***He has a way of fading into the background.***" This is perhaps the most pertinent point of the movie: Freeman was able to fade into the background and better survey all that was taking place around him. This is what is meant by, "the spook who sat by the door." He listened, observed, learned and then – he applied it.

The second man is hardly listening to the first one talking about Freeman's low-key approach, responding instead that, "Yes, they do make good athletes."

The same brother who tried to explain "the art of tokenism" in an earlier scene is among the others who come to Freeman's room that evening to pick him up so they can go check out the city (Washington, D.C.). Freeman turns them down politely, informing them that he is going to stay in and study. The tokenism expert calls Freeman an Uncle Tom and said that if Freeman's high scores would not have raised the grading curve so high, "there would be three times as many of us here." He then asks, "What kind of Uncle Tom are you?" Freeman replies, "the same kind as you, I guess." Freeman informs the brother that, "I doubt that any of us here were picked because of our militancy."

The brothers want to go party and Freeman wants to study. One insinuates he's an Uncle Tom. Freeman sent the grading curve up. "What kind of tom are you?" "Same kind as you I guess." Then, the brother says, "I think you'd be happy with a mop in your hands," to which Freeman replies, "Like your mama?"

The brother acts like he wants to fight, but Freeman slowly and calmly takes off his glasses and simply informs him: "You don't want to step outside with me. Because baby, I would kick your ass." The other brothers grab up their angry colleague and get out of Freeman's room. Let us deal with Freeman's concept of playing the dozens and see just how true the statement was.

Recall that the brother alleged that Freeman would be happy with a mop in his hands. That statement was not true, but was meant to be an insult. But the fact is, many black people mopped floors for white folks and didn't like it one bit (a point addressed in a later scene). So when Freeman says, "Like your mama?" this was no insult. Like that man's mother, a person can have a mop in their hands and not have to be happy about it. While the statement sounded insulting, it was actually a backhanded slap at the facts. Like that brother's mother, Freeman would NOT be happy with a mop and in fact, that brother's mother would not be happy, either.

They guys who left hadn't been out on the town for a month, and neither had Freeman. So after they leave his room, Freeman grabs his jacket and heads for a bar in the black community where, as one white man observed earlier following surveillance, "he (Freeman) seems to be most comfortable."

Freeman goes into town on his own and checks out a black club. Lovely Paula Kelly sits at the opposite end of the bar, so Freeman sits down, orders a drink and then sends one down to her as well. In vintage fashion, she accepts the drink and then walks down to where he is seated. She's a pro and he's a trick looking for a good time. They negotiate and then head over to the hotel. This of course, was during a time when such transactions were clean, no worry about AIDS, about the woman being a man, about being jumped in the room, or any of that. Just a clean sexual transaction between a trick and a ho.

Once in the room, they're relaxing prior to sex, and he tells her she reminds him of someone he saw in a book, a queen. "All you have to do is give me my bread, you don't have to talk that trash," she says. He tells her she resembles "a queen from Dahomey" and explains that, "Dahomey was a great nation in Africa. I've got a book with a picture – you look just like her. You two could be twins except she wore her hair different. It was kind of natural, the way it grew. You would look good like that."

They had more than sex that night. She learned something from Freeman. First of all, it was obvious that she rarely received compliments and the ones she did get were not of the quality of being confused for an African queen. The impact that Freeman had on her when he saw her again (it is implied that they began dating after that) could be see in her change of hair style, dress and overall demeanor. More on this point later. The next day represents a turning point.

On the agenda is martial arts training. The entire class is paired off as the master teacher (an Asian) throws them and teaches them how to take a fall. After all that is complete, the class is dismissed – all except for Freeman. When the others are gone, with only the instructor still present, the white boy, Calhoun, tells Freeman,

> Mr. Freeman, I don't think your people belong in our outfit. I
> don't have anything against the rest of the group – they just don't
> measure up. But you – I don't like.

Freeman replies, "I don't understand, sir." But Calhoun is not finished,and continues:

> Well, I don't like your phony humility and I don't like your style.
> Now, this is a team for men, not misplaced cotton pickers …

Freeman says, "yes sir." Calhoun then tells Freeman,

> Stow the yassah boss! It doesn't work on me. I'll give you a
> chance. Just go up to the office and resign. Otherwise, we fight.
> Now your black belt matches my own, so you won't be able to
> whine 'brutality,' equal opportunity – you people claim you
> want.

Freeman proceeds to kick Calhoun's ass – knocks him out by employing a sleeper hold, and Calhoun has to be revived by the Asian teacher. Later, it is revealed that Freeman had been studying judo for years – on his own. This is an important point.

The thing that makes us great is what we do in our daily lives that prepares us for life. In the case of college, for instance, not only was I intellectually superior to students and teachers alike, but more importantly I knew it. That is the key. But to know means you have a responsibility to act on what you know. That is why so many people I attended school with are wasting away working to empower a system that hates their guts. That is why, for the most part, so many of them are a waste of skin and oxygen. They believe in the white man more than he believes in himself. Tom as they might, they come to class and race to the back of the classroom. I, on the other hand, was hunted. My weekly column in the student newspaper, cracking on peckerwoods and dealing with race issues, made me the number one target.

White instructors would try to catch me off guard and it got to the point where I would trick them into calling on me. I would pretend to be nodding off, or I would give a gesture to make it appear that a question that to the class had surprised me. Being the cowards that they were, they'd call on me, hoping I wouldn't be ready. But I was – not just to answer the question, but to take over the class and use the hatred of the students in my favor. The more questions they asked or more attempts they made to debate me, the more likely I was to wear that ass out. As Ernie teaches, "where much is known, much is required." What Freeman did to that judo instructor, I intellectually did to white faculty and students alike at UNO.

During all this we find that Freeman has a woman who visits him. It's his wife and he loves her. She's a casework supervisor back in Chicago, and he convinces her to stay the night one evening. Hold this point because we will refer back to it in a few minutes.

The next morning it is clear that Freeman is the last man standing. The other brothers did not make the cut. Still, the CIA interviewed people and ran security checks. They even interviewed the Dahomey Queen, and she had nothing but positive things to say about Freeman's character and activities.

During the final oral examination, Freeman is asked a question about guerilla warfare, and he answers it, drawing from his studies and training:

> "To live off the country. To rely on nothing in the ay of logistics
> or supplies which cannot be obtained easily and simply, whether
> legally or illegally."

Final checks showed that Freeman was someone who should be accepted into the ranks of the CIA. The final report on him showed that he checked into a colored hotel and spent most of his time in the ghetto ("he feels comfortable there"), and not only did he study judo privately, but he had been involved in civil rights while a college student (where he met both Joy and Dawson) and there were no hints of homosexuality. (Oddly enough they screened for homosexuality when one of the biggest faggots of all time, the cross-dressing J. Edgar Hoover, was running their rival agency, the FBI while all this was taking place). They interviewed Dahomey Queen and she simply gave him a glowing review and said, "He's one of those quiet cats that people just don't mess with."

The conclusion? "Well, like it or not, we're integrated," says one white man. And that proves that they knew, all the while, that they were NOT, but having no blacks around represents a comfort zone for THEM.

Freeman's in. And for five years, he performs photocopying and those kind of tasks. He's got access to top secret information as he works in his assigned area in the 3rd sub-basement.

After a while, he has won over he trust of everyone has he bides his time. One day he is asked to give a tour of one of the areas. The people want to make sure that the CIA has, indeed, "integrated." He comes upstairs and meets a group of senators, who he takes on the tour. As he leaves, one senator gives Carstairs and his fellow administrator a thumbs up, congratulating him on what he sees as "real integration." When the senator leaves, Carstairs says, "Integration in action. We can put him (Freeman) out in the reception area."

This particular scene is relevant because it reflects the mentality of white people, both then and now. To those people, one black person among ten whites is integration; to them, placing a black man or woman in a high visibility cubicle (like they do at Mutual of Omaha) is a signal to those who come onto that floor or into that area that the company is an "equal opportunity employer." Most of these people are so shallow and stupid that they do not realize that, for one thing, they piss off most of the black people who have to occupy these areas. And secondly, most progressive minded people can clearly see the tokenistic treatment because white men have been doing it to white women for years.

The concept of "integration" never addressed the issue of power. And as many of the old folks will tell you, integration destroyed black businesses. So starved for white acceptance were our "leaders" (Martin Luther King among them) that they gave up the farm. We traded eating, sitting and shitting next to white folks for our black-owned taxi stands, our black hotels, our black movie theaters and so on. And we pay for that tragic mistake to this very day, even as some cities try to return to the times when "Black dollar days" was a year-round reality.

One day Freeman returns home to find out that his wife wants to leave him. She has met a doctor and she tells him about it. He is understanding, informing her that, "I knew this day would come sooner or later." He is amiable about it and they make love one more time before calling it quits for good.

Joy's role was not as fully developed as the others, but it is clear that she is a money-grubber and an opportunist. Almost every scene she appears in during the movie has something to do with money and a job. She has obviously been screwing around behind Freeman's back and latched onto a brother who made more money. That is why Freeman's two guesses were, "a lawyer or a doctor?" He knew. And Joy, because she chose material wealth over someone who cared about her, would regret this decision.

Freeman continues to go about his job and his low-profile. One day at lunch he's talking to the head man, known as "The General," at lunch, and he's been there just over five years. The first thing out of the General's mouth is, "you're a credit to your race."

"You're a credit to your race" and "Some of my best friends are black." White folks, to this day, continue to believe that these two statements are complimentary! Why, because at the base of both statements is the white man setting himself as some kind of standard. For him to deem someone a credit is a statement of paternalistic arrogance, as if they have the right to deem single blacks as "credits" because, as the statement implies, most blacks ain't shit. "Some of my best friends are black" again sets whitey as the standard; the fact that some of his friends are black is supposed to convince the unwitting black that he is somehow 'liberal' or "accepting" or "more understanding."

Moving along, check out the following exchange:

> GENERAL:
> No denying your people are great in sports.
> FREEMAN:
> Thank you sir, but we still have along way to go.
> GENERAL:
> Right, there's still a cultural gap to be closed. A question of
> evolution, of course it would take generations. In the meantime,
> you people must earn respect by serving the country – Freeman,
> your people must SERVE!!!

As the white man, the General, utters these words, a black bartender is serving them both drinks and as the white man pulls out a cigar, Freeman beats the bartender to the lighter used to light the white man's cigar. This is a symbolic scene on several levels.

First, both black men are doing just what this white man suggests – serving! And that is how most black men are judged: what kind of "service" they can provide. "Did you serve in the military?" "Who are your people?" (wanting to know if his parent or grandparents have a record of "serving"), "Where do you work"? ("what fellow white man do you work for so I can check you out before extending this credit").

Secondly, what these white folks occasionally forget is that no one has "served" more often and for a longer period than those who were held in slavery. These people want to believe that they are the ones who built the agricultural economy that made this country rich; they want to dupe themselves into accepting that "blacks sold themselves into slavery" or "you should be glad we got you because look at Africa now." They actually believe this bullshit. Their Bible, their intergenerational mis-education of their young, and their continual contortions of historical reality are attempts to make them appear moral when, in reality, they are the most evil collection of people in the history of the world. Crack a book – you'll see.

Shortly thereafter, Freeman decides its time to pursue other interests and submits his resignation. He tells his supervisor that he wants to return to Chicago to "show his people the way." He tells him that he has decided to take a position with the Social Service Foundation. He says he's going to "help his people to help themselves" and that he's going to "use what I've learned here." All of these statements are true – just not in the way the white man anticipates. Later the white boys are talking and to them, Freeman is simply leaving because the new job in Chicago offers more money. With them it's always about pay – but Freeman is more concerned about MAKING white folks pay than he is about personal wealth.

The fact is, Freeman used to be a member of a gang called the King Cobras when he was young. On his way into Chicago in a cab, he happens to have a driver who remembers the days when the Cobras were a dominant force on the streets, and the gang is now 30 years old and still going strong. At that time Freeman's nickname was "Turk." The recreation center they used to hang out in front of, the Cobras now own it. Freeman has a job, he's got a place to stay and now its time to get back on the streets and put together his "army."

A few weeks later, presumably, Freeman is out on the streets making some rounds. He stops in a restaurant and runs upon Miss Duncan, the mother of Shorty Duncan. When he asks how Shorty is doing, she answers "fine," although it is clear that Freeman knows better. She adds that he just bought her a new color television. She acknowledges that he runs numbers and that he's hooked on drugs, but adds, "he ain't no real junkie" and that he only shoots "twenty or thirty dollars a week. That ain't no real habit."

To this day black mothers defend their sons, no matter what they do it seems. I've heard black mothers claim that their sons are not involved in anything when, in reality, these little assholes are running more drugs than Walgreen's. And then there are the mothers who defend these punks because they are getting paid;

he'll give her a diamond watch or buy her a car. In some cases, she's his best customer. So if it was taking place when this movie was made, and its still taking place now, then it's not just a "freak occurrence" or a "quirk;" it is part of the reality of drug dealing and drug consumption that, for some reason, the scholars and the legal people don't want to deal with.

Freeman looks at her as she consumes her meal. "Did he ever think about finishing high school?" Freeman asks. "No," Ms. Duncan explains. "He don't want no parts of school. You know how those teachers are." "What's he gonna do with no education?" Freeman asks her. Ms. Duncan looks at him and says, "Mr. Freeman, you know ain't nothin' out there for us."

Ms. Duncan is not totally wrong. Even back in the early '70s there were teachers that would ignore black kids or harass them. These kids were "pushouts," but were blamed for dropping out because they were trifling. But when you go to class every day and you get treated like shit, or you have to listen to "Little Black Sambo" or "Black Pete," it's enough to make you skip class, skip school and/or eventually drop all the way out. But you left because you were made to feel unwelcomed in the first place.

What comes to mind is what Malcolm X talked about in his autobiography, and a fourth grade teacher he had named Mr. Ostrowski. This is a conversation that young Malcolm was having with a teacher that he naively trusted:

> "Well, yes, sir I've been thinking I'd like to be a lawyer." Lansing certainly had no Negro lawyers – or doctors either – in those days, to hold up an image I might have aspired to. All I really knew for certain was that a lawyer didn't wash dishes, as I was doing. Mr. Ostrowski looked surprised, I remember and leaned back in his chair and clasped his hands behind his head. He kind of half-smiled and said, "Malcolm, one of life's first needs is for us to be realistic. Don't misunderstand me, now. We all here like you, you know that. But you've got to be realistic about being a nigger. A lawyer – that's no realistic goal for a nigger. You need to think about something you can be … It was then that I began to change – inside. (Malcolm X, 1965 :38).

How many black kids were "changed" and ended up in prison (as Malcolm did) because the Omaha Public Schools took its time "caring" enough to begin thinking about diversity in the schools?

So Ms. Duncan understood the problems but didn't believe they could ever be changed. She submitted the system and never thought about what she might be able to do to try to alter it. Because so many black people adopted this attitude, it is left to those who see the reality or race relations to have to do something about it. Freeman was one of those kind of people.

Freeman leaves the restaurant and walks down to the corner where Shorty is selling dope.

They greet one another and Freeman starts right in. "Shorty, the word on the vine is that you're not making your payoffs to the cops." Shorty, not surprised that Freeman knows, says, "That's just a rumor, Turk." Turk is now concerned: "Mind if I give you a little advice?" Shorty tells him, "Yeah, go ahead." "Why don't you just quit dealing altogether?" Turk asks. Shorty tell him, "You know I can't do that, Turk. It's survival." Turk has the following to share:

> You ever stop to think what would happen in these streets if we
> cut off the flow of drugs altogether? White folks control YOUR
> neighborhood through drugs and you dealing?

Shorty asks Turk if he came down there to give him a sermon, and Freeman answers truthfully, "No, no sermon, Shorty. I just thought I'd ask."

But a key to the preceding exchange is that when Freeman asked Shorty if he could give him some advice, Shorty didn't answer the way many of today's young people would have answered. Shorty showed an interest in hearing what Turk had to say. And even though he didn't agree with it, *he listened nevertheless.* Of course, that was then, and this is now.

Turk walks off and later that night, he's down at the pool hall, a hall that is now owned by his former gang, the King Cobras. Three of the main brothers – Do-Daddy Dean (known as just "Daddy"), Pretty Willie, and Stud Davis -- walk past the other tables and straight over to where Freeman is shooting pool by himself. They inform him that he's playing on THEIR table.

> FREEMAN:
> You know who I am?
> COBRA #1:
> Yeah *flunky,* we know who you are
> FREEMAN:
> Let's go out in the alley. This wont' take long.

Even though they say they aren't going into any alley and that he, Freeman, is going to leave by the front door, Freeman ignores them, puts down his cue and walks out the back door to the alley, anyway. As Freeman exits you will notice the words "Black Power" scrawled on the wall and a picture of Malcolm X – not Martin Luther King – hanging on the wall. At any rate, the three Cobras look at each other and, what the hell, they decide to go out there where they think they're going to beat Freeman's ass.

They thought wrong.

Freeman has no problem subduing them as they come into the alleyway. He grabs one of them and pulls the gun on him. The Cobra tells him, "Next time, social worker, we have us a piece, too." Then, Freeman begins taking them to school intellectually:

> Shut up and listen – big time bad ass Cobras! Poppin' away at
> the pigs from the rooftops during the riots last summer? Oh yeah,
> I know what you was into. With 22 rifles and pistols? Did about
> as much damage as a mosquito to an elephant's ass. What did
> you expect to hit from that range with those weapons at night?
> You may as well have thrown those damn pieces at the pigs. You
> really wanna mess with whitey? I can show you how.

And so it begins.

They begin with hand-to-hand, then explosives (just as he learned, he teaches others), demolitions, street assault practice, rifles and molotovs.

During the Molotov instruction, Willie has concerns: "What are we doing messin' around like a high school chemistry class? Anybody can make explosives like this." Freeman replies, "Okay Willie, you go order us some plastique and detonators from Marshal Fields." The group has a good laugh. Now, the education, as Freeman explains that,

> Everything on this table can be obtained easily from a drug store,
> a hardware store or a medical supply house. When we can get
> sophisticated equipment, we'll use it; but we don't rely on it. We
> live off the land. We match technology with spontaneity and
> improvisation. Men against machines, brains against computers.
> Now if you don't think it can work, you check out Algeria,
> Kenya, Korea and the Nam. Can ya dig it?

Willie responds with, "I understand, man. It's cool." Again, one black man willing to listen to and learn from another. Today, or so it seems, ***this is a rarity.***

The next day he's spending time with another Cobra. This time they're on the waiting area near the "El" train. It's time for more revolutionary education:

> We found out in the country how difficult range estimation is.
> But in the city, the problem is simplified. A city block is 250
> yards north to south, 150 yards east to west. Lamp posts are a
> standard 30 yards."

This means that there are reference points all over and, as Freeman further explains, "The buildings act as a funnel for the wind, you can fire on zero windage." He tells he Cobra to go back and run the information down to the sniper teams and that he will meet them later.

That night Joy comes over for a visit. She is impressed with his nice digs and the fact that he is now making so much money. She says that ever since the War on Poverty started, social workers were making good money. She notices that he has changed (for the better) and that her marriage is crumbling – she claims the man she married has changed that maybe she "should have waited" for Freeman. He tells her, "It's to late to talk about that now. You already have a husband." She tells Freeman she's seen their old friend Pete Dawson, and that he's back from California. Freeman is glad to hear that and apparently knows exactly where to locate Dawson.

Remember that Dawson was able to contact her first, implying that they had been in contact prior to that. I will share a theory that I have about Joy and Dawson later in this analysis.

That night, Freeman enters a club with two women on his arm, and doesn't have to look very far before he spots Dawson. He leans over and they greet each other. He asks Dawson to come over to where he and the two ladies are sitting, so Dawson says something to the woman he was sitting next to and joins the threesome on the other side of the club.

He informs Freeman that he was in California teaching a 15-week seminar on inner city riot control, what he calls "the Chicago police department approach to street gangs." Freeman finds it funny, but Dawson reminds him that he was a former war lord (for five years) with the Apache street gang. Freeman is now impressed, observing, "hoodlum turned cop." That night they party together with the girls and it is clear that they have immediately rekindled their friendship that they once had while in college and before that, on the streets of Chicago. Freeman makes a toast to Dawson: "Here's to old friends re-discovered." Dawson puts up his glass, looks over at the women and says, "And here's to new ones. Freeman leans back: "Now tell me about this new job …"

Next day, it's back to training. The next phase -- learning how to steal.

As they sit in a circle around the room, the mention of stealing gets a chuckle from most of the brothers. Freeman replies, "Yes sir, I know you're all experts – in stealing from your black brothers and sisters! Now you will learn how to steal from the enemy." He teaches them: "Remember, a black man with a mop, tray or broom in his hand can go damn near anywhere in this country. And a smiling black man is invisible." These words should be heeded by the Uncle Toms of Omaha and Milwaukee who believe that smiling in the white man's face brings them favor. He doesn't even see them, let alone respect them.

In the next scene a brother undergoes a test, using what he has been taught. The target is the president of Chicago Edison, who is in his office on the phone as a brother, posing as a window cleaner, walks into the office. The man is a collector of antique smoking pipes, and they are on his desk. While this white boy is on the phone, the brother not only steals the pipe rack with the antique pipes in it, but also steals another one on the way out – using nothing more than the white man's negligence as a screen.

The invisible man. Ralph Ellison put it well, and it is a reality in American society and part of the "self-deception" that white folks are engaged in to this day. They train themselves to see what they want to see. They believe that black people in the ghetto are happy because, to believe otherwise, would place them in a state of on-going paranoia. They train themselves to believe that "busing" worked although failure was evident. But the thesis of "sitting next to whites will mean that blacks will learn" continued on and helped their system and organized crime rake in billions.
They render us invisible when its convenient because we are their most glaring contradiction; we are a reminder that despite their Internet, space ships and hi-tech visions, ***they have yet to solve their race and color hang-ups.***

The next scene is one of the most instructive in the film, and it deals with skin color, education and attitude.

Freeman goes over to visit Willie, a high yellow brother with straight hair, who could actually pass for white. Willie's apartment is adorned with the amenities of that time, black liberation flag, several African masks on the walls and so on. Freeman and Willie sit across from each other, Freeman on the couch and Willie in a chair. They are both drinking tea.

Freeman has heard that Willie is a writer, so he begins by telling him, "We need a propagandist. So you're the Minister of Information. I want you to set up a group, use whoever you want." Willie asks him if he wants posters or music or pamphlets and Freeman says he can use it all, "anything – as long as you talk to the people in the language they understand." Freeman asks for an outline of his strategy in two weeks, but Willie says, "One week, man, that ain't no problem." "Beautiful," Freeman replies.

As they talk, Freeman tells him, "I hear you're still registered at the university." Willie acknowledges the fact, explaining that he has to take a few courses, "To keep that brad coming from home." Freeman asks him, "you ever intend to get a degree?" Willie says, "Now what do I need with a status symbol?" Freeman is somewhat taken aback and fires back, "That's all it is to you?" Willie tells him, "For a black man in THIS country? What else is it?"

Then, Freeman shares the following story with the younger man:

> You know how my grandmother learned how to read? Along
> with me. You remember those reading primers? [Dick and Jane]
> … When I first got into those books, my grandmother used ot
> wait for me to come home from school so she could "help" me
> with my reading. And she would follow the whole thing, line for
> line. Then one day – I don't know why, I just read the line
> wrong, and I realized she couldn't read. And I went into the
> bathroom and I locked the door. And I cried. And every day after
> that I ran home so that my grandmother could help me read. And
> man, the first time I saw her really read … Get your education,
> boy, she used to say, because that's the only thing the white man
> can't take away from you. She was right."

This passage should be read to every black child in kindergarten and first grade in this country. From grades kindergarten through third grade, you learn to read; from fourth grade on you read to learn. Freeman, as a child, knew the importance because his grandmother emphasized it, although she herself could not read. She was like my father, who quit school after fifth grade to go to work and take care of his brothers and sisters. But he knew the value of education and all ten of my brothers and sisters graduated from high school. He would accept nothing less.

Willie understands that the moral is for him to take his education more seriously, but he asks another kind of question by beginning, "You know, I can't figure you, man." Freeman asks, "What's to figure?" Willie explains, "I mean, what you in this for? You want power, you want revenge – what is it?" Freeman looks at him and responds, "It's simple, Willie. I just wanna be free. How 'bout you?" And Willie says, "So do I – and I hate white folks." This is where Freeman gets to explain why motivation is so important, and it also puts the lie to the claims made by Wickham in the introduction about what was going through Greenlee's mind. Freeman explains, as follows:

> Hate white folks? This is not about hating white folks. It's about
> loving freedom enough to die or kill for it if necessary. Now you
> gonna need more than hate to sustain yo' ass when this thing
> begins. Now if you feel that way, you're no good to us, and
> you're no good to yourself.

Actually, both of them were somewhat correct. Stanford (1970) wrote, "Without the courage to despise the enemy and without daring to win, it wil be simply impossible to make revolution and wage a people's war, let alone to achieve victory" (p. 31). So while I understand where Freeman is coming from, I feel its better to be indifferent toward the white man – to have no real feelings either way – than to hate him. Hate involves passion and could lead to an emotional attachment. But there is no doubt that white folks and their system, are one and the same. You can't hate the root of the tree and not hate the tree itself, as Malcolm taught.

Then, the follow-up: "You ever kill a man, Willie?" Willie says he has not. So Freeman tells him, "I have. In Korea. And when you spill a man's guts in the gutter, you see how fast hate disappears. Unless you like killing, and I don't think you will. Now some of the Cobras will – Studs will." Willie asks, "Why Studs?" Freeman says, "Because he's a killer. He doesn't know it yet, but he is."

Now, the subject again shifts. "I have another job for you, Willie," Freeman says. "What's that?" Willie asks. "We need money. So I had the bank job cased. The only thing about it is I can't have the bank job connected with the Cobras." Willie asks, "How you gonna do that?" Freeman tells him, "We need Red Beads, Benny Rooster, Po' Money, J.T., Johnny and Tom – and you lead the team."

Willie gets up from his chair, obviously pissed off:

> All the yellow niggas, right? Look man, I am TIRED of that. I am not passing! I am black! Do you hear me, man? I am black, do you understand? I'm a nigga, do you understand? I was born black, I live black and I'm gonna probably DIE black because some cracker that KNOWS I'm black, probably better than YOU, nigga, is probably gonna put a bullet in the back of my head!

And that's how the scene ends. But Willie understands the logic later on, because in the next scene is the bank robbery itself, a robbery pulled off smoothly, and although shots are fired to scare the employees and customers, no one gets killed.

The guys escape in a white van, and Freeman is across the street at a gas station making sure everything runs smoothly. The fellas take the van and turn into an alley after they change clothes. They then pile into a white Biscayne and make their escape. As they're riding down the street, they hear the report on the radio that a bank has been robbed and that more than $300,000 was taken. The report says that six white men were responsible.

The next day Freeman meets Daddy at a basketball court, and their comparing information on the city-by-city organizing of the revolution. They agree that the key is to go to various cities and locate a gang like the Cobras. They have to have "tight discipline" and, remember: "no junkies." Freeman pinpoints the cities of Boston, New York, Philadelphia, Detroit, New Orleans and Los Angeles.

Daddy says, "They got some ba-a-a-d brothers in New Orleans." Freeman replies, "You got that right."

And Freeman also reminds Daddy that there will be monthly reports until contact is made and then after that, weekly reports. If anybody gets busted in a street hassle, they recruit in the prisons and "we replace them" (the brothers who got taken in).

That evening, Dawson comes over to visit. Joy is already there and seems extra happy to see him, as **she gives him a hug**. As he takes off his coat, Joy is seated and Freeman fixes him a drink. Dawson is boasting about his son and how good an athlete the kid is turning out to be. **Joy asks Dawson if there is a chance that he and Eileen – obviously his ex-wife** – will ever get back together again. He tells her no, he didn't think so, and how tough it is to be the wife of a cop.

He is seated and, having dipped into Dawson's business, Joy realizes it is time to head out. She goes to the back and gets her coat and Dawson asks Freeman, **"Can't cut her lose, can ya?"** Freeman contemplates and answers, "No, she knows me too well." Joy comes from the back with her coat on, says goodbye. **She then kisses Dawson goodbye – on the lips** – and then kisses Freeman more intimately before she leaves. Nothing is made of it, but in a later section of this book, I address this "strange" triage.

After she's gone, the two fellas can't wait to get their coats on so they can head out to some parties. Dawson tells him that he was going to tell him (Freeman) about two chicks he came over to tell him about before he saw that Joy was there. These two are very close and this scene is established to show just how far back, and how close as friends, they really are.

A few nights later, I assume, the last finishing touches are being put on the revolutionary training. There's a meeting of the key brothers at Freeman's place: Willie, Daddy, Freeman and Stud. Freeman shows them some new needles and tells them to put needle marks in their arms to imitate being junkies. "Put needle marks in your arms and keep 'em fresh," Freeman instructs. "And no pig is going to bust you for the things we'll be doing as long as you got those tracks."

As everyone sits down, Freeman pontificates, and the thesis of the book and gist of the movie becomes clear:

> We are gonna get our own. Stop begging for crumbs … What we
> got now is a colony. What we want to create is a new nation. In
> order to do that, we gotta pay a different kind of dues – freedom
> dues.

The creation of a "new nation." Max Stanford offered similar sentiments when he wrote, "The whites have had to use terrorism in order to control black

America. By the proportion of the population – in the South especially – Afro-Americans constitute a nation within a nation" (p. 38).

Moving on, following an impromptu comedic race relations skit between Daddy and Willy, where they imitate a slave and a former slavemaster, Freeman sums up: "What y'all just played out is the American Dream. *Now, we're going to turn it into a nightmare.*"

Right on.

That night they raid a military arsenal – scaling fences with unity and precision. Hey cut open internal fences and drive in a bus to rip of guns, ammunition, grenades, etc. They steal a military jeep, and as they leave, the jeep follows with some of the fellas riding in the back. The bus comes to a red light and as Daddy sits waiting for the light to turn green, an elderly white woman walks up, totally dismissing the "Out of Service" sign on the side of the bus. She bangs on the door demanding that Daddy open it and just then, a cop car pulls up. "This one's off duty lady, can't you read?" one cop asks. "Catch the next one." The light turns green, she backs off, and the cops take off, not aware of the huge cache of guns that was in the bus right next to them.

At a warehouse the Cobras unload the goods. Somebody says, "You know this gonna hit the headlines." Freeman disagrees: "No, it won't hit the papers at all. It might give other people ideas. BUT, this place will be swarming with CIA and FBI." Willie asks, "Do we go underground?" Freeman replies, "No, They'll be looking for everybody EXCEPT us. You see, this took brains and guts, which we don't have, right?" They move the stuff out to various hiding places.

At the pool hall the following day, Daddy tells Freeman, "Some of the boys is 1-A for the draft, man. What we gonna do if they get caught, go underground?" "Yeah," Freeman says. "If they can beta it, they should. BUT we recruit every 'Nam vet we can get. Right now I'm trying to recruit Dawson as a double agent." Then the following conversation, one none of us should never forget, takes place:

> DADDY:
> Turk, you think we can win?
>
> FREEMAN:
> In guerilla warfare, the winning is in not losing. When you sleep
> on the floor, you can't fall out of bed.
>
> DADDY:
> Then what we trying to do, man?
>
> FREEMAN:
> Fight whitey to a standstill. Force him to make a choice between
> two things which he seems to dig most of all. There is no way the

U.S. "There is no way the United States can police the world and keep us on our ass at the same time without our cooperation … When we revolt, we reduce it to a simple choice: whitey finds out he can't make either.

DADDY:
Well, the Cobras is ready. What about the other brothers and sisters?

FREEMAN:
Their choice is when we start. If they don't follow our program and turn us in to the cops, we lose in a week. But if they support us, then its hit and run, harass and hound, and we can paralyze this country.

DADDY:
Yeah, right. Trainin' done started already in nine cities, and five groups are combat ready – plus US.

FREEMAN:
Right. And by next summer we should be able to hit the ten largest urban complexes in the United States.

Cut to scene, a dark alleyway with a lone brother running at top speed. Two cops are giving chase. One in the open on a dark side street, the cops open fire and shoot the brother twice in the back. There is a late night call to Freeman, who is in bed – with Joy (probably in more ways than one). Daddy is on the other end: "Look like a riot getting' ready to start. Pigs burned a cat." "Who?" Freeman asks (as if he knows every nigga in Chicago). "Shorty Duncan. *Yeah, after all the training, looks like the shit is going to start over a jive-ass pusher.*"

They decide to meet at the Cobras pool hall. Freeman is up and putting on his pants as Joy wakes. He tells her, "Cops shot a kid, looks like it could be trouble." She tells him, "Don't get involved," but he replies, "Gotta go, don't worry about it," he assures her.

Out on the streets black folks are pissed, and are milling around. Freeman sees Dawson, and he's been telling the brothers to cool it. One of Freeman's social work colleagues, Burt, is there with him and he tells Burt to go down to the drugstore and use the phone, and round up all the social workers. Obviously, this was a time when social workers cared about, and were involved in, the lives of their clients. Not so today.

Freeman runs over to break up a fight between two brothers, one of them older and in a suit. Freeman lays down the line to the one he grabs:

Wait a minute! Listen to me, man! What is this gonna do, man?
You got a wife that's worried about ya, you got a job, you get
busted you gonna lose it. Plus, you one of the few people that's
got a job to lose!"

The brother understands but yells, "Man, this has got to stop some time or somewhere. We ain't animals!" The brother walks off.

The crowd is about to disperse, peacefully, when two cops – one black and one white – come in with police dogs, german shepards. Dawson shouts, "Get those dogs outta here! The black cop says, "The captain sent me up here." But Dawson doesn't give a damn: "I'm telling you to get 'em out. Now I'm in charge. You know how these people feel about dogs!" The cop says, "But I got my orders!" Dawson pulls out his pistol and tells the cop, "Just move 'em, or I'll kill 'em." The cops take the dogs away, but now the crowd has its own ideas. Dawson tells Freeman and Burt, "We'll have to move back as soon as I can pull my men out."

As Burt shakes his head and mutters, "Oh man, it was gonna be alright," Dawson sends up a flare. The cops, Burt and Freeman begin to pull back as the crowd gets rowdier. Then – a full-fledged riot!

Cars are overturned, and several of the brothers are jumping on cops. Cops are beating people with their batons, and Dawson gets a chance to see how cold these white cops are. He comments, "They had to bring those god damn dogs in here!" An overturned car is set afire as more cops arrive. Then, shots are fired from all over the place, including the rooftops. An empty three-story building is firebombed as the paddy wagons are bought in. A fire truck arrives and people throw rocks and pop cans at the firemen to prevent them from putting out the fires.

The next day, Freeman pulls up to talk to the curb in his red sports car. He's there to meet Stud. "Boys ready?" he asks him. "Been ready," Stud says. It is established that primary and secondary targets have been checked twice a day, and the guns are "oiled and ready." Stud is impatient, but he also knows the rank of command and respects Freeman's orders to "wait." "You're the man," he acknowledges. "Right," Freeman replies.

An overhead view of the riot-torn street can be seen, cars on fire and military vehicles dot the landscape. No people on the streets, but the National Guard is in full swing, sweeping the streets and randomly arresting anyone. Freeman approaches Dawson's car and is invited in. He takes the passenger side and the following important conversation takes place:

FREEMAN:
How long since you been in bed?

DAWSON:
Not since the riot started.

FREEMAN:
That was three days ago, man.

DAWSON:
Yeah, I know. I cat nap when I can.

FREEMAN:
When the National Guard come in?

DAWSON:
Late last night. All white.

FREEMAN:
I noticed.

DAWSON:
The people didn't dig it when they woke up this morning and found the troops were here.

FREEMAN:
What do you think they'll do?

DAWSON:
I can't see them trying to fight the army.

FREEMAN:
They didn't mind fighting the police.

DAWSON:
Yeah. I never seen 'em like that.

FREEMAN:
Maybe that badge has put distance between you and them.

DAWSON:
Oh yeah, yeah I forgot. The pigs over here and the people over three and never the twain shall meet, huh? Hey man, I grew up down here, too, and I know these people. And there was some good people out there in the streets the last few nights – not just hoodlums like they say in the newspapers.

FREEMAN:
In a scene like this, **_anybody_** can get involved.

DAWSON:
But that's only gonna make it worse. We have to maintain law and order or we might as well be back in the jungle!

FREEMAN:
Dawz, the ghetto *is* a jungle, always been. Understand? You cannot cage people like animals and not expect 'em to fight back some day. There has always been an army of occupation here, with police badges and uniforms. You and me – a cop and a social worker – we are the keepers of this god damn zoo!

DAWSON:
The streets have to be safe.

FREEMAN:
Safe for who? You're here to protect property, not lives.

DAWSON:
Well, that's what it's all about, isn't it? You worked hard to get what you got, didn't ya – and you wanna keep it, just like I do …

FREEMAN (angry):
Bullshit! Listen, you think because you got a badge, and I got a couple of degrees, there's a difference? Do you know what white folks cal people like you and me in private? Nigguz, Dawz. Nigguz.

DAWSON (sees the transformation in Freeman):
Hey, hey, hey. Haven't heard you talk like that since we were in college.

FREEMAN (after a long silence, realizes he's blowing his cover):
Well, I'm sorry, man. Maybe the last three nights been a little bit much. I got a board meeting – I gotta go reassure white folks. Let's go get something to eat, okay?

DAWSON:
Okay.

Freeman, normally super-cool, lost his cool but for a few seconds two times. His conversation with Dawson was one time, and Dawson logged it in his mind. The second time would be in a conversation later on, with Joy. And Joy would also see it. Keep this in mind.

Freeman tells Dawson he's here to protect property and not lives – and Dawson agrees. That says a lot about his role as a cop, doesn't it? So many black people selling out so much for so little. Again, Nathan Hare:

> There also remain those among us who too easily sell (or rent) ourselves out to our oppressor, who sincerely believe that money is just about everything and so are strongly inclined to do just about everything for money, selling our souls for a small-time job, a small-loan grant, for two bits and a bowl of chili beans. It is one thing to own money but quite another to be owned by money. Money is a medium of exchange for many useful commodities, but we may yet discover that the best things in life may still be free and that, in contrast to the sellout, the martyr may even be blessed (p. 5).

The statement about "selling" or "renting" out black people is also made by Greenlee during an interview on the DVD, and is somewhat a cliché in black nationalism. Even Karenga, in his handbook, the Quotable Karenga, had a statement about "if the white man's buy a Negro, he can always rent one."

At any rate, a few days later presumably, the Cobras invade a local radio station. All are masked, but it is clear that it is Freeman who gets on the air as "Uncle Tom." As he's doing his thing and other brothers in the station are tying up the DJs, other Cobras are setting a bomb in the office of the mayor of Chicago. On air, Freeman lets out the following message:

> "This is Uncle Tom – Commander-in-Chief of your black freedom fighters of North America, bringing you the latest news from your fightin' black underground. Hang on, brothers and sisters, liberation is near. In just a few minutes at precisely 3:00, we will demolish the lavish offices of the mayor of white Chicago 'cause we don't have a mayor even though they do count our votes several times to elect him every four years.
>
> Remember brothers, despite the lies about an assassination attempt on the mayor which will appear in the white press, this time we blew the mayor's office at night, when he was home, to announce the beginning of our war of liberation. I'd dedicate this program to the National Guard, but we're fresh out of hillbilly music. And according to the press and television, the Guard spends all its time playing basketball with kids and helping old ladies cross the street. But we know better, don't we?
>
> We know about that 14-year-old girl that the trigger-happy Guards shot last night and the people they beat up, and the black

> businesses they destroy, don't we? It's almost time [he begins
> counting down from 10 seconds] … Blast-off! And the mayor's
> office is now air-conditioned, courtesy of the black freedom
> fighters of Chicago. And the message is this: pigs and National
> Guard have to go immediately, if not sooner. If they haven't left
> by midnight Sunday, we will kick them out. Whitey, go home.
> We don't want you in our neighborhood, either, and we will
> defend our nation.

Why the mayor's office (other than the reasons stated by Freeman)? Because it falls in line with what Max Stanford wrote in 1970: "The mayor's areas should also be completely demolished. This keeps the lower elite section of the capitalist ruling class isolated in the suburbs for days without communication with the outside world" (p. 33).

By the time the cops arrive at the radio station, the Cobras are gone and the DJs are all tied up. A point here.

While the Cobras used propaganda to the fullest, there are other reasons to deal with the communications system in this country. One of those ways is clearly delineated by Stanford, who explains:

> In the process of revolution, the mass communications system
> would be the first to go. Why? Because the enemy's populace
> and supporters rely on the mass communications system to know
> how to relate to events. By destroying the oppressor's
> communication system the revolutionary nationalist creates a
> vacuum in the oppressor's apparatus and isolates him form his
> machinery. Also, it sets the oppressor at a disadvantage because
> he will have to attempt to rebuild his system in the middle of a
> battlefield (pp. 32-33).

Why did Freeman have to be the one whose voice would be associated with Uncle Tom and the freedom movement? The fact is, it is this fact that would tip Dawson off later in the movie. While propaganda is important, it is also important to control, as much as possible, who is getting your message. Here in Omaha with Channel 22, we give out a lot of information to our brothers and sisters, but white boys – including members of the City Council, County Board and so on – are listening in, too. Even the local media listens in to steal story ideas.

The next day there is a press conference called by the National Guard's leader, Colonel Evans. Evans sells woof tickets about what all they are going to do, and so on. "We will leave when things are back to normal – with them on the bottom and us on the top." He doesn't explain who "them" is, but it is safe he means ALL black people, not just the Cobras. Meanwhile, the Cobras are about to make him eat his words. They come directly to the headquarters of the National Guard and catch the Guard leader sitting at his desk watching a western on television, voting against the Indians.

They mug him, bind and gag him and lay him on a table. Daddy proceeds to paint the white man's face black, leaving his lips white. Now he looks like one of those minstrels from "Bamboozled." At any rate, Willie mixes some LSD in some tea and they force feed it to Evans. A short time later that morning, the streets are empty and two Guardsmen see Evans riding on a bicycle, high as a kite, face blackened and wearing nothing but his boxer draws and a t-shirt. They stop the bike and Evans says, "Hi men, how are ya? I just met with the most marvelous bunch of niggers!" As he prepares to repeat what he said, a bullet tears through his chest from a rooftop. The two Guardsmen take cover.

That night a larger army truck is coming down the road. A Cobra throws a Molotov near the truck, just enough to get the gun happy soldiers to come running out. And that is just what they do, more than 20 of them, with their rifles. They give chase, and run into a trap; bullets rain down from the third floor of an abandoned tenement as a firefight ensures, but the Cobras get the best of the soldiers. Then, the Cobras take off on foot – hit-and-run, hound and harass. The president of the United States orders The 82nd Airborne called in for reinforcements, as backups for the "beleaguered Guardsmen," as the media reports it.

The General and Carstairs meet in a hotel suite in Chicago. They have the following conversation:

> GENERAL:
> You've been here since the beginning, Carstairs. How does it
> look to you?
>
> CARSTAIRS:
> General, it couldn't be worse.
>
> GENERAL:
> We have elite troops out here now against untrained black
> fanatics. The whole thing should be over before the weekend.
>
> CARSTAIRS:
> Those troops are facing a highly trained underground guerilla
> army. They have military weapons and they know how to use
> them. The commander of those elite troops says he can put this
> thing down in a few days.
>
> GENERAL:

You disagree?

CARSTAIRS:
Yes I do, sir. They're a first class fighting unit.

GENERAL:
You've prepared an option for me?

CARSTAIRS:
Yes sir.

GENERAL:
And … ?

CARSTAIRS:
We have three. Root them out one by one, starve them out by siege, total evacuation of the black population.

GENERAL:
Evacuation?

CARSTAIRS:
The first is too costly in lives and equipment and neither evacuation or siege would work.

GENERAL:
Why not?

CARSTAIRS:
General, we sealed off the ghetto for three days last week. It paralyzed the city.

GENERAL:
Paralyzed Chicago?

CARSTAIRS:
Chicago is more dependent on black labor than one would think. Ninety percent of the garbage collectors are colored. Sixty percent of the hospital workers are colored; 60% of the bus drivers and 80% of the postal workers. So, although the concentration --- the **detention** camps occurring under the 1950 Subversion Act are ready, we can't put them to immediate use.

GENERAL:
Your recommendation?

CARSTAIRS:
We can end it alone, sir.

GENERAL:
Yes?

CARSTAIRS:
The Russians obviously have a top agent prop man here. Find
him, destroy him, and you have disorganized, ignorant Negroes
to deal with.

GENERAL:
Cut off the head, the body dies.

CARSTAIRS:
Exactly.

GENERAL:
Alright Carstairs, get right on it. I'm going back to Washington.

To interject here before moving on. In the preceding conversation, Carstairs recites statistics on the importance of black labor to Chicago. In November of 1970 in his article in **Black Scholar,** Max Stanford wrote that there are a number of powers that black people in this country have. Among them, he wrote, "is the power to hurt the economy. With black people creating mass chaos – especially in the major urban areas in the North – and disrupting the agricultural setup in the South, the economy of the oppressor would come to almost a standstill" (p. 30).

It appears that now, some thirty years later, things remain essentially the same in terms of percentages. Could this be the root reason behind black unemployment? Surely we are qualified for these bullshit jobs we apply for. But could it be that they keep us out of the workforce so that they will not become dependent on our presence in those jobs?

Carstairs shakes hands with the General and then leaves. As soon as the door is closed, the General puts his drink down on the desk and enters into the side room. He looks at someone, pulls out his wallet and counts out money: "Honey, I'm going back to Washington. Why don't you amuse yourself here for a few days? You be back by Sunday, huh?"

The woman is – the Dahomey Queen! She's dressed form head to to in African gear, her hair close cropped and she says, "Sure baby. I'll find something to do in Chicago. It is clear that Freeman's influence had as much influence on her as it had on Joy and the other women he's had in his life.

But several points about the preceding conversation before moving on.

First, the concept of "elite troops." The white man's "elite troops" are self-described and self-named. Could they do the job on the streets of New York, Chicago or Los Angeles? Hell no! If one of those so-called elite soldiers bumped into a junkie and broke his crack pipe, that junkie would beat the living shit out of that white boy! Look at what those Iraqui janitors, steet cleaners and carpenters are doing to the so-called "American military machine." You're elite only if, as the definition informs us, you are "A group or class of persons enjoying superior intellectual or social or economic status." These white boys only have superioir social and economic status because they are in a white society that rewards whiteness. But when it comes to intellect – *we shall see what we shall see.*

Secondly, the belief that the revolution would be quashed "before the weekend." Sound familiar? This is the same bullshit that we heard from these American "military leaders," including Colin Powell, as they were supposed to go into Iraq in the name of "Iraqi Freedom." Then, when they found out it was more difficult than they thought, they came up with "Shock and Awe." After they continued getting their asses kicked by people they were supposed to "defeat in a month," they now realize they underestimated their opposition and went into Iraq "unprepared." The movie then, was prophetic when it comes to the white man's arrogance when it comes to the battlefield.

Third, the issue of "options" and those "detention camps." A brother named Samuel F. Yette wrote a book called, ***The Choice: The Issue of Black Survival in America.*** Yette was born in 1929 in Tennessee and was hardly a militant. But when he was working for the government, he came across some documents and some information, and then he wrote The Choice. Having read the book, I can tell you that the main contribution that he makes is the information that he provides regarding the Internal Security Act of 1950 and guess what? This Nebraska hick and former Governor, Roman Hruska – whose name now stands on the side of the new Federal building in downtown Omaha – was one of the people that presented the bill before the Congress.

The Internal Security Act of 1950, also known as the McCarran Act, was actually put together by McCarran and this senator from Minnesota named Tidings. Tidings was ill and couldn't present the bill on the floor one day, so Hruska did it for him. The thrust is to lock up any group of people that might be considered a threat to America. Yette, in his 1971 classic (mysteriously out of print) shared with the nation what was going on behind closed doors. And check this out: after his revelations were published in The Choice, Yette – who was a Washington correspondent for *Newsweek* magazine – he got fired. The point is, he didn't just stand by and watch and read about what was being said or planned about his people: he did something about it.

Three years before that, in 1968, another brother – John A. Williams wrote a novel called, ***The Man Who Cried I Am.*** It was billed as an autobiography, but the book deals with a brother who has left America because of the racism and more importantly, the book deals with white folks' fear of the black power movement. But here is what it has to offer: a few pages about the existence of "The King Alfred Plan" and the way that this spread all over the nation truly proves how powerful we, as blacks really are. But the promotion of it represents the kind of "guerilla" approach that Greenlee talks about later in this book.

It seems that Williams took the pages about King Alfred out of his book and photocopied them. He then left those pages, outlining the plan to control black people, on the seats of buses all over New York. The word spread like wildfire about this "conspiracy" to get black people. Uninformed black folks were talking about it from coast-to-cast, and even Gil Scott Herron mentions it on one of his albums. In the minds of most black people, King Alfred is real; I believe it is. But the information describing it, which came from the torn out pages of a 1968 novel called ***The Man Who Cried I Am,*** and was nothing more than a plan to market his book through word of mouth!

These two books are both important in understanding how far the white man will go to incarcerate or "detain" people, in general, and people of color, in particular (lest we forget the illegal internment of 110,000 Japanese during World War II, of which 90,000 were American citizens).

The fourth point made between Carstairs and the general was the issue surrounding the power of black labor and how it "paralyzed" Chicago.

Again, we have to go back to a point that was touched on earlier: is black unemployment a result of some "adjusting" that was made to decrease the dependency that white America had on black labor? Surely, the dependency has decreased with the influx of immigrant labor, the advent of technology and the reduction of what was considered "menial labor" and of course, more blacks being locked up and therefore not being hired into the workforce because they're ex-cons. But the power of black labor in America was so strong at one point that Black Scholar magazine dedicated several issues to the topic, and it is clear that black folks here in America come from a tradition of labor. If we know it, then "they" know it.

Fifth, the racist belief that a white man would have to be calling the shots for black people in order for there to be a successful revolt against this system. This was the same thing that Charles Manson thought as part of his "helter skelter" plan: take a wallet from a raped white woman and leave it in the black community. Call the cops and they'll start attacking blacks which will, in turn, trigger a riot. The blacks will win, but get this: we'd be so stupid after we won, we'd have to find a white man to tell us what to do. And that was supposed to be when Manson would come out of hiding and take over. Ain't that a bitch? (And don't forget, Manson's **Helter Skelter** was published in 1969, three years after Greenlee wrote the book and four years before the movie -- so this was the same and context in which Spook was written).

In the next scene Dahomey Queen has located Freeman. "How'd you find me?" he asks, inviting her into his pad. She says she found him in the phone book, but then proceeds to let him know that she's got a new benefactor and she's stopped hustling. This white man who is paying her has "a thing for black meat" and he's somebody who he (Freeman) knows. Of course, it's the general.

She tells him that the money's good and that she used it to purchase herself some property; a smart sister and a message in that line as well. She tells Freeman that he knows who the trick is, and the following conversation takes place:

> FREEMAN:
> I do?
>
> DAHOMEY QUEEN:
> Yeah. You used to work for him. You know, you his **nigga!** All the time he be saying if all of us niggas was like you, it wouldn't be nooo trouble. First, I thought he was talking about somebody else.
>
> FREEMAN:
> So?
>
> DAHOMEY QUEEN:
> So they out to get Uncle Tom.
>
> FREEMAN:
> Well, what makes you think I know anything about Uncle Tom?
>
> DAHOMEY QUEEN:
> I'm not saying you do, but you know Chicago and I don't
>
> FREEMAN:
> What am I supposed to do?
>
> DAHOMEY QUEEN:
> Warn him. Tell him they out to kick as and they ain't playin'.
>
> FREEMAN:
> One thing (hands her a drink). Why you stickin' your neck out?
>
> DAHOMEY QUEEN:

I'm black, ain't I?

FREEMAN:
Yeah. Yeah, you are, baby (takes her lighter and lights her cigarette). Who's in charge?

DAHOMEY QUEEN:
Carstairs.

FREEMAN:
What are they up to?

DAHOMEY QUEEN:
They plan to get inside, find out who this Uncle Tom is, and kill him.

FREEMAN:
Cut off the head, the snake dies. Do they know who Uncle Tom is?

DAHOMEY QUEEN:
They think he's some guy from Russia.

FREEMAN:
They would.

DAHOMEY QUEEN:
You want me to see what else I can find out?

FREEMAN:
No. Wait I minute – two can play at this infiltration game. Find out all you can, but don't pry. I'll have somebody contact you in Washington. Baby, be very careful. And don't contact me again **unless** I get to Washington.

That night there is more warfare. Cobras on rooftops force a jeep off the street (as in Iraq today) and the shooters converge on the white boys who are on the ground. One young white soldier, wounded, asks, "Why me?" The masked brother says, "'Cause it's war, honky!" The Cobras scatter as the cop sirens get louder. They get away using the rooftops.

Again, Max Stanford called it correctly in his 1970 piece on guerilla warfare. What Greenlee bought to life in book and film form, Stanford had outlined. For instance, he wrote,

The concept if lightning campaigns conducted in highly sensitive urban communities … The new concept is to huddle as close to the enemy as possible so as to neutralize his modern and fierce weapons. The new concept creates conditions that involve or not. It sustains confusion and destruction of property. It dislocates the helpless, sprawling octopus. During the hours of day sporadic rioting takes place and massive sniping. Night brings all-out warfare, organized fighting and unlimited terror against the oppressor and his forces (p. 32).

The next scene features an argument between Freeman and Joy, a classic argument between a grass roots thinker and revolutionary, on the one hand, and a bourgeois capitalist on the other:

FREEMAN:
Why should you feel threatened by the freedom fighters?

JOY:
Because I am – and you are too!

FREEMAN:
How?

JOY:
You know how! With all the progress we've made over the last few years. We'll be wiped out of this thing isn't stopped soon. I heard even your Foundation is on the way out.

FREEMAN:
Well, no. They decided to increase the budget *and* the staff.

JOY:
Yeah?

FREEMAN:
Yeah.

JOY:
Well, my husband was dismissed form the hospital. And he was the first and only Negro on a white hospital staffing this city!

FREEMAN:
Well, what is the connection between your husband and the freedom fighters?

JOY:

Dan, that is the whole point! Innocent and decent people are suffering because niggas who know noting but hate and revenge!

FREEMAN:
Its all the niggas' fault, right?

JOY:
Don't romanticize those people, Dan. They're not beautiful.

FREEMAN:
Only by contrast.

JOY:
Dan, those freedom fighters are murderers!

FREEMAN:
If didn't figure to be long before those *niggas* realized that you don't have no win throwing a *brick* at somebody with a *gun!*

JOY:
Dan, whose side are you on?

FREEMAN (catches himself just as he did earlier with Dawson):
Your side. (Joy stares at him suspiciously). We're in the same bag, making the best of a bad scene.

Too late! Next scene she's having lunch with Dawson. And she's spilling her guts!

JOY:
I think he's mixed up with those black freedom fighters.

DAWSON:
Dan? You gotta be kiddin'?

JOY:
I'm sure of it. We were talking and – I don't know – for a minute he was like he used to be.

DAWSON:
Yeah. He was something else when he was in college. And that was before all this became fashionable.

JOY:

He was defending those animals – then he caught himself. He
said all the right tings, but it just wasn't *him.* Just wasn't the man
I know.

DAWSON (mumbles something about a source of intelligence.
Then says):
His gig takes him all over the ghetto. Look, I'll check it out.

JOY (uncertainty in her voice):
Pete – I am doing the right thing.

As I discuss in another section of this book, Joy and Dawson were more than
"friends." This concept of meeting for lunch and kissing on the lips and her
wondering if Dawson and his ex were going to get back together and Dawson
asking Freeman "can't get her out of your system" – this spells "affair" in my
book. I liken it to these white people who live next door to each other in suburbia.
The woman comes over to visit the lady next door and she and the husband hug –
or kiss. Or the couple comes over for a night of cards and each one kisses the
other's spouse. Fuck all that; "hi, what's up," and that's that. What starts off with a
hug or a kiss can end up being an "affair" when people get too "tight." Freeman
could see the long range plan but couldn't see what was going on right under his
nose.

That evening, presumably, Freeman enters his place and closes the door.
There sits Dawson with his gun drawn, pointed directly at Freeman.

DAWSON:
Just put your coat down, right there.

FREEMAN (walking up to the upper tier of the room where
Dawson stands)

DAWSON:
Come on Uncle Tom, come on!

FREEMAN:
Uncle what?

DAWSON (shoves Freeman against the wall):
Spread your feet out, come on! (Pats Freeman down, police
style)

FREEMAN:
What is this? Some kind of joke, man?

DAWSON:
Yeah, it's a joke. The joke is on me! I been looking all over for Uncle Tom and here you are under my nose. Cool Dan Freeman: only digging sports cars and bread, good clothes and chicks. Beautiful cover, man.

FREEMAN:
Hey man, think about it. I mean really, think about it. Would I risk all this for *that?*

DAWSON:
Oh you don't have to worry about that, man. I got enough evidence to take you in and that's what I'm gonna do.

FREEMAN:
What evidence?

DAWSON:
Them tapes, man! Them Uncle Tom propaganda tapes that you cats spread around the ghetto. Well, I listened to 'em over and over again. And its you, Dan. It's your voice.

FREEMAN:
You gotta be crazy.

DAWSON:
We'll see whether a voice print proves whether I'm crazy or not.

FREEMAN:
Now what?

DAWSON:
Now what? The scene is over. But one thing, one thing. Are you working with the Commies like they say? Who's behind you?

FREEMAN:
How come there's gotta be somebody *behind* me?

DAWSON:
Oh come on, man, don't put me on. No. The FBI says it's the most sophisticated underround movement in the western hemisphere. The work of an *expert!*

FREEMAN:
And expertise is the white man's monopoly, right Dawson? *Well I am the expert!* I spent five years flunkyin' to become a expert!

DAWSON:
This gun makes *me* an expert.

FREEMAN:
You're a big man with that gun and that badge. You know Dawz,
you wanna have it both ways; you want a pat on your head from
whitey, and you want the love and respect of the people, but you
can't be with the people without betraying that badge, and you
can't be a cop without betraying your people, you hypocrite!

DAWSON:
You think nobody else feels the way you do? You think you're
the only nigga with a sense of outrage?

FREEMAN:
Well then, hit back! Join us! We can use you! We've got
undercover people on the force!

DAWSON:
The force?

FREEMAN:
That's right.

Dawson;
Who?

FREEMAN:
Nobody with your rank. Come on and join us, Dawz!

DAWSON:
You're using *kids!!!*

FREEMAN:
Who else am I gonna involve? People like you and me? Uh-Uh.
The kids are our only hope. I got to them before they got jailed or
killed or turned into Dawsons! And now they'll do anything to be
free.

DAWSON:
Who said you were free, man?

FREEMAN:
Well, Dawz, even on the wrong side of your gun, I'm a lot freer
than you are.

A few words regarding the previous exchange.

When Freeman tells Dawson to "hit back" at the system, he is clinging true to revolutionary philosophy – the enemy of your enemy is your ally. Stanford put it simply: "Urban guerilla warfare is an ever-growing concept as a solution to the end of oppression among the Black masses in America. As racists continue to attack Afro-Americans, blacks will resort more and more to guerilla warfare. This will bring a confrontation between the black and white races here in America" (p. 32).

Back at Freeman's place, a fight ensues. Freeman uses his karate skills and flips Dawson down the short stairway, but rolls down with him. They gather themselves to their knees and Freeman grabs a knife from a table. As he guts Dawson, Dawson fires his gun. Dawson drops dead, and Freeman is seriously wounded.

Freeman goes to the phone and summons Daddy and the other officers. Freeman changes from the dress shirt he had on into a dashiki, to hide his stomach wound. Daddy, Stud and Willie arrive a short time later and the following important conversation-information exchange takes place, after Daddy goes over to the body and says, "It's Dawson!"

> STUD:
> Hey man – Dawson's your main man. That would be like me
> killn' Daddy.
>
> FREEMAN:
> Yeah. Maybe one day you'll have to kill Daddy – or him, you.
> You think we're playing games, killing white strangers? There
> are a lot of Dawsons out there and some of them gonna try to
> stop us. But anybody who gets in between us and freedom has
> got to go. Now that's anybody. You got the Airborne out there
> now. And forty percent of those troops are black. Maybe they'll
> help us, maybe they won't. But in the meantime, if you hesitate
> with any one of them because they're black – just once – you'll
> be one dead Cobra.
>
> Now if you're out simply to pay them kind of dues, then you get
> out and go back to don' nothing,' but don't tell me who I killed,
> and what it cost me to do it.

Daddy, Stud and Willie stare at Freeman, taking in what he said. They are confused, but they understand:

> FREEMAN:

Now you get him out of here. Get him out.

WILLIE
Right, Turk.

Daddy grabs a spread off the bed to wrap Dawson's body in.

FREEMAN:
It is now condition red. All fighters in the field. Alert our
compounds everywhere. Remember: don't quite 'til you either
win or you die.

Great concept. But I am more inclined to fight to live! As one brother put it,

A few years ago it was the fashion among black militants to
speak of a willingness to die for freedom. Today we know that
revolution is more about living than it is about dying, that in
these times black men are dying for a freedom that does not
necessarily follow in their wake. We are coming around to the
notion that we must live, live to fight and fight to live and all that
that implies, in whatever direction (Hare, 1970: 4).

Willie, Stud and Daddy carry the body out the door as Freeman shuts it
behind them. The shit is on, and Freeman is hurt bad, more than likely dying from
the gunshot wound

As the movie ends, the President of the United States has declared a state of
national emergency. Freeman knows that the revolution is underway. He gives a
silent toast as he glares out the window.

This, friends (and enemies) is a magnificent movie. But as in all things, there
are a few minor conceptual flaws or concerns that I have.

In the opening scene, the Senator is being advised by two women. Why?
This defies logic in a heated campaign. The white man is not only a racist, but he's
also a sexist. Perhaps Greenlee, who heavily favored the brothers in the
revolutionary planning, wanted to show that the white woman was as involved as
her man is in our oppression. But what about the brainy sister who was helping
him to dupe us?

The role of sisters in the movie was, for the most part, positive albeit on
different planes. Dahomey Queen was a prostitute, but Freeman saw something in
her and helped her develop her potential. She was "black" all along (in terms of
color) but didn't use her consciousness until he worked with her. Then, she was
able to use her former profession to make money, acquire property, and play an
important role in the revolution.

Joy, on the other hand was nearly the polar opposite. She could care less about Africa and, in fact at one point referred to the freedom fighters as "animals." What was that all about? Materialistic, aspiring and fine, she wanted financial security at any cost. And she wanted a man who had the same values as she did; Freeman didn't cut it because he cared too much about his people. That's why, in my view, she was so attracted to Dawson. All three had gone to college together so she knew the both of them. Freeman probably cared so much about both of them he never suspected that something might be going on. But I do.

And what happened to the brothers who didn't make the final cut following the CIA training? Returned to the streets, more than likely. But why didn't they use what they had learned the way that Freeman did? But this brings us to a major flaw in the entire process. Furthermore, by having gone through that process, wouldn't they have been the prime suspects once the revolution went down?

Why would the white man pick "the best?" Sure he needed a token, but if the person chosen was only going to do flunky's work anyway, what difference did it make? Wouldn't it have been more effective to pick someone who wasn't as qualified as Freeman and then use that man's flaw to justify why no blacks are ever chosen? That is what they usually do. Or why not pick TWO finalists and observe how they relate to and interact with each other and their white colleagues? Whoever is the biggest tom would win. But this is perhaps too complex for the message that Greenlee was trying to make, which I believe was that our best and brightest are not always going to roll over and be lap dogs for peckerwoods. Some of us know what needs to be done and as importantly, are fully aware of what this system has done to US and our ancestors. And some of us ain't gonna forget it.

The scene where the six finalists confront Freeman in his room and Freeman, in response to being asked if he was an Uncle Tom, says that he doubts if any of them were chosen based on militancy. No, they were not. But this represents a contradiction linked to the previous one. They were chosen because they were smart and reliable as far as whitey was concerned. And yet, they didn't make the cut. White racism is the reason for them being cut, but the racist system could have put them to use in other areas, could they not?

Here's how I see it: the white man's criteria for even being selected was a tommish criteria from the get-go. He picked the "safe negroes" or the ones that he felt would be no threat to his system. Then, he puts them through tests where they are exposed to hi-tech and guerilla warfare. Then he turns them away. Wouldn't it have been safer to keep them around? With all that information, even the biggest Uncle Tom is going to put it to use somewhere down the line, just as many Vietnam veterans did when they got back. This seems to be a breakdown in Greenlee's logic.

The scene where Freeman's wife, Joy, tells him that she wants a divorce because she's met another man goes a little too smoothly. Or, perhaps I'm judging it based upon today's standards. Freeman was too understanding; if he suspected something was going to happen, why did he not nip it in the bud? After all, the best revolutionaries are those with no close ties, no one that the enemy could use or get to, right? As a revolutionary then, it was HIS obligation to create distance between himself and Joy – not hers.

And here's another thing about this scene. Joy agrees to make love one more time and the first thing she does is take off her wig. But why is she wearing a wig? When she takes it off, her own lovely black hair is evident and, in fact, its pinned up. What's up with that?

Here's another point for your consideration: if Freeman was such hot shit on the streets of Chicago when he ran with the King Cobras, how come this didn't show up on his jacket when the CIA was running their security checks?
In another scene, as I alluded to earlier, Joy comes over to visit Freeman and she tells him how her marriage is crumbling. Then she informs Freeman that Pete Dawson was back from California. I wonder about the relationship between Joy and Dawson. The three of them went to college together, and Dawson knew how to get in contact with her despite the fact that she was married to someone else. Then, in a later scene when the three of them get together at Freeman's house, she prepares to leave and as she heads for the door, she kisses Dawson – on the lips. After that she kisses Freeman goodbye, a more intimate kiss of course.

And Freeman, the great thinker, strategist and visionary, couldn't see it.

In another scene, Daddy and Freeman are going over some fine points of the revolution and the cities that will be targeted. Freeman pinpoints the cities of Boston, New York, Philadelphia, Detroit, New Orleans and Los Angeles. Daddy says, "They got some ba-a-a-d brothers in New Orleans." Freeman replies, "You got that right," Freeman agrees.

This falls right in line with what Stanford wrote in regard to these urban areas:

> The complex outside the cities like New York, Detroit, Chicago, Buffalo, N.Y., Lansing, Mich., Philadelphia, Cleveland, etc. , are convenient for revolutionary nationalists. The destruction of such complexes could be achieved by stationary mortars or mortars from an automobile (p. 33).

I'm not so sure about New Orleans. My people hail from Louisiana and I've done some research on the state and its main city. In fact, my thesis for my second Master's degree dealt with elitism in five states, and Louisiana was one of them (the other four were California, Minnesota, Nebraska and Pennsylvania). It was during my research that I encountered just how crooked and nepotistic the New Orleans Police Department was – and still is. A major sting of cops back in the early 1990s found all kinds of shit going on: legalized hits using cops as assassins, drug dealing by cops, shakedowns of drug dealers, the whole nine yards.

Now true, this is the cops that are dirty. But in New Orleans, the whole city is about freakishness and frolic, with Mardi Gras being its main tourist attraction. The cops are therefore in on whatever is going down – but so are a lot of the brothers and sisters. How, therefore, could these party people be any "badder" than the brothers in L.A., Philly or Detroit?

And there are not enough southern cities in the initial wave. The south is key, or at least that is what Stanford believed when he outlined his plan for revolution. Check it out;

> Birmingham, Ala. Is the main industrial complex in the South. Being that the social, economic and political structure is divided into two different categories, our partisan war of national liberation must have a dual front. The South is a rural area, but because of communication, terrain (basically flat) and transportation (highways), it takes on a semi-urban character … Blacks constitute at least 45 per cent of the population of Louisiana, 59 per cent in Mississippi, 45 per cent in Alabama, 50 per cent in Georgia and 55 per cent in South Carolina … The Southern Front would shift quickly from guerilla to mobile warfare … (pp. 33-34).

Perhaps the time limitations imposed by the film prevented Greenlee for discussing more details about the importance of the southern urban centers and their potential contributions.

Well, there's some food for thought. When you hear people like Bernie Sanders and these young white folks going around shouting about "political revolution," they don't know what the hell they're talking about and the system isn't even taking them seriously. To make such pronouncements is an act of sedition and black men have been murdered and jailed for such statements. Talking about revolution is one thing, but playing with the word is like playing with matches: if you don' t know what you're doing, you'll get burned.

"A CHILD BY TIGER": A REVOLUTION OF THE MIND

In this book on various types of revolution, it is imperative that the "revolution of the mind," the one that prepares the would-be revolutionary for combat with his enemy, be explored.

This story was written by a white man who was hardly a revolutionary of any kind. The short story was published in the year 1937. How he got his information I have no idea, but more likely than not he read the real story in a newspaper and then fabricated the rest. This is not really the point. The point revolves around the conclusions that he arrived at, conclusions that are based on erroneous assumptions, wild conjecture, and bullshit. I will prove these charges as I analyze the story, point by point.

Bear in mind that the story begins with the first stanza from a poem, The Tiger by William Blake, which simply says,

> Tiger, tiger, burning bright
> In the forests of the night,
> What immortal hand or eye
> Could frame thy fearful symmetry?

It boils down to a living thing doing what it believes and feels it has to do. This type of thinking is the thinking of the would-be revolutionary. We shall deal with this later in this analysis. In the meantime, Wolfe begins his short story, thusly:

> One day after school, twenty-five years ago, several of us were
> playing with a football in the yard at Randy Shepperton's. Randy
> as calling signals and handling the ball. Nebraska Crane was
> kicking it. Augustus Potterham was too clumsy to run or kick or
> pass, so we put him at center, where all he'd have to do would be
> to pass the ball back to Randy when he got the signal.

Young white boys innocently playing ball in their yard. Most would say that this is the way it should be and in white American culture such a scene is representative of the prototypical American lifestyle. White kids, healthy, taken care of, well-fed without a fear in the world. And yet in this idyllic setting, right across the way, what do we have? As you will see there is a section called "Niggertown," an area where black people are forced to reside, a segregated section of the city. Today, in 2016 the situation remains pretty much the same; every major city, from Oakland to Omaha, from New York to Dallas, as a black community, a veritable "pocket of poverty" as the white city planners call it.

I mention this fact at this juncture to establish, from the get-go, the duality of American society. While these white kids play their football games and frolic, there are black kids and black families who are struggling to make ends meet. And that difference has nothing to do with merit, but a whole lot to do with white racism. This will be a recurring theme in this book because for the most part, Wolfe makes references to the symptoms but he – like most white men – are too arrogant and careful to deal with the actual "disease."

Continuing with the story:

> It was late in October and there was a smell of smoke, of leaves, of burning in the air. Nebraska had just kicked to us. It was a god kick, too – high, soaring punt that spiraled out above my head, behind me. I ran back and tried to get it, but it was far and away "over the goal line" – that is to say, out in the street. It hit the street and bounded back and forth with that peculiarly erratic bounce a football has.

The kid named Nebraska was hardly given than moniker because his white parents loved or knew about the Nebraska Indians. No, he was named after the conservative hick state in the middle of the country, one that is a prototype for segregation. There are only about 60,000 black people in the state and 50,000 of them live in Omaha. Of that number, more than 90% reside in an eight-square mile area on the northeaster sector of the city which is known as "North Omaha." In other words, "Niggertown." Art imitates life either directly or indirectly, does it not?

For instance, Hall and Wood in their book about "the South" write that, "Niggertown Marsh was the original name of a Civil War era rural marsh community that is notable for being one of the first recorded settlements in Florida, run and maintained entirely by freed slaves, or Freedmen, after the end of the U.S. Civil War." They continue by writing that, "The settlement, in Highlands County, was founded by a man called "Nep". The larger area of the settlement was named Niggertown Knoll, next to it being Niggertown Marsh. In the early 1990s, the original names were viewed as offensive and the public authorities stripped the names from public record and map" (Hall & Wood, 1996). But look how long it took to get the name changed; and even though it is clear that "Niggertown" was not the official name of the area even during the times in the Wolfe story, white people and black people knew what it meant, knew why it was given the name and the boundaries were as formal as any boundary on a zoning map.

The youth continue their frolicking:

> The ball rolled away from me down toward the corner. I was running out to get it when Dick Prosser, Shepperton's new Negro man, came along, gathered it up neatly in his great black paw and tossed it to me. He turned in then, and came on down the alleyway, greeting us as he did. He called al of us "Mister" except Randy,

and Randy was always "Cap'n" – "Cap'n Shepperton." This
formal address – "Mr." Crane, "Mr." Potterham, "Mr.' Spangler,
"Cap'n" Shepperton pleased us immensely, gave us a feeling of
mature importance and authority.

Let's look at the racial and racist implications of what was just put on paper by Thomas Wolfe.

To begin with, the reference to Prosser being referred to as "Shepperton's new Negro man." The writer knows the importance of words, and he phrased it this way on purpose. He could have said that Prosser was the Shepperton's "new nigger," but he didn't, and why not? Because he's building up the story and showing the "acceptability" of Prosser as a resident, worker and obedient flunky. He's "a good nigger" and therefore there is no reason to regard him as such (not to his face, at least). This is the white way and Thomas Wolfe, the author, well knows it.

Secondly, the black man's hand being called "his great black paw." Even though Wolfe is navigating the racial waters the best way he can, there are certain "racial facts" that white men will always claiming. Among these is the belief that black men are beasts. You can hear it today when they announce sports, making on-going animalistic references to a black man being in "beast mode," or black running backs constituting a "stable," or a coach "reining in" a black athlete. And in this case, the hands become paws because humans don't have paws – only animals do. And on a psycho-sexual level, many women believe that the larger the hands, the larger the dick. And the black dick is the one thing that the white man has always feared and envied.

Point number three is the fact that Prosser calls these boys "Mister" and one of them "captain." Such references by black men to white men and boys has a long tradition, mainly in the South but surely applying all over the country back in the day. In Richard Wright's autobiography, *Black Boy,* he writes about the time he took a job at a clothing store that was run by racists and the white men made fun of black customers every day. At one point Richard's bicycle gets a flat tire after he makes a clothing delivery.

A group of young white men offer to let him ride back to town on the side of their car. When Richard neglects to call one of the white youths "sir," they smash a whiskey bottle in his face, causing him to fall from the speeding vehicle. He walks back to town. The white man John Howard Griffin who dyed his skin black and wrote *Black Like Me* also shared similar stories. A black man knew how fickle white man and boys were and therefore few would ever neglect to refer to them as "sir," "mister" or some other undeserved honorific title.

Fourth and finally, the feeling the boys got as a result of the references made by Prosser in point number three. When you are but a lad and a grown man is calling you "mister" and "captain," and you know that such a recognition is based on the fact that you are white and as such, somehow "superior," this stays with you. That is how white privilege in America is maintained: white people getting unearned and undeserved kudos simply because they are colorless.

One explanation for this was offered by the late Dr. Frances Cress Welsing in her "Cress Theory of Color Confrontation" when she wrote:

> … the initial psychological defense maneuver was the "repression" of the initially felt thought or sense of inadequacy – **being without color** and, of secondary importance, being in deficient numbers, both of which were apparently painful awarenesses. This primary ego defense of repression, was then reinforced by a host of other defensive mechanisms. One of the most important was a "reaction formation" response whose aim it was to convert (at the psychological level) **something that was desired and envied (skin color) into something that is discredited and despised** (Welsing, p. 35 – emphasis added).

Sure, it's just a theory. But it goes a long way in explaining how a worldwide majority can feel comfortable getting the kinds of kudos and compliments that they receive. These kids had to know that they weren't about shit. They had to know that the black kids who lived in nearby "Niggertown" could kick their asses in boxing, basketball, football and any other competition. But they feel happy in their little enclaves where, when they get out on the dance floor for instance, they won't have to compete with black people. That's why those assholes called the TV show featuring "The Fonz" and other other racists, "Happy Days." In essence, the concept of "Happy Days" describes a world with no niggas around.

Oh, and one more thing before moving on:

> **The whites desiring to have skin color** but being unable to achieve this end on their own, said in effect, consciously or unconsciously, **that skin color was disgusting** to them and began **attributing negative qualities to color** and especially to the most skin color – **blackness** (Welsing, pp. 35-36 – emphasis added).

And I accept much of what she says. These people realize that most of what they have is based on deception, brutality and various violations of their word. They know that their religious beliefs are a joke and that their culture exists because of what they're "borrowed" from other people. They hide much of their history from their children because they know that if their children knew how callous the white race was and still is, they (the children) would turn on them (even as they are beginning to do now in 2016). Knowing this, we can now better frame the situation of these young people and their perceptions of and relationships with this "negro" who they have befriended:

> "Cap'n Shepperton" was splendid! It had a delightful military association, particularly when Dick Prosser said it. Dick had served a long enlistment in the United States Army. He had been a member of a regiment of crack negro troops upon the Texas border, and the stamp of the military man was evident in everything he did ...

Prosser was probably undergoing some regular harassment if he was working on the Texas border. Those are some of the most racist peckerwoods that there are. Not only because Texas is a southern state, but because it is a state of stupid people. I saw them, interacted with them and know this for a fact. From their elected officials on down, black and white, the majority of the ones I met were borderline idiots. But this is a different time which means that things were worse back then during the times of the story. Prosser was a good soldier and the kids liked that because it meant that he was disciplined and that he fought for this country. Even a young white boy knows a "good nigga" when he sees one.

These kids watched Prosser in the same way that the white male adults, then and now, homoerotically observe and worship the black man's physique, his movements and his style. Again, witness their comments during sporting events, both then and now. Take note of the following:

> It was a joy, for example, just to watch him split kindling. He did it with a power, a kind of military order, that was astounding. Every stick he cut seemed to be exactly the same length and shape as every other one. He had all of them neatly stacked against the walls of the Shepperton basement with such a regimented faultlessness that it almost seemed a pity to disturb their symmetry for the use for which they were intended.

The white people during that time had a saying: "an educated black man is a good field hand, spoiled." This is the same mentality that these boys share: they describe the physicality of Prosser and they admire (envy?) it. That is because he is no social threat to them, because he hails from a racial grouping that they (white boys) have no reason to have to interact with, and because, when all is said and done, he's just "another nigger." But he is one who they liked because he lived in a space in the basement of the Shepperton house. That made him "safe" and therefore approachable; so much so they even recalled and could describe the condition of the room that Prosser lived in:

> It was the same with everything else he did. His little whitewashed basement room was a spotless as a barracks room. The bare board floor was always cleanly swept, a plain bare table and a plain straight chair were stationed exactly in the center of the room. On the table there was always just one object: an old Bible almost worn out b constant use, for Dick was a deeply religious man. There was a little cast-iron stove, and a little wooden box with a few lumps of coal and a net stack of kindling in it. And against the wall, to the left, there was an iron cot, always precisely made and covered cleanly with a coarse gray blanket.

The black man was orderly and clean. And one thing that white folks, young and old alike, truly admire (or require) about a black man is that he be deeply religious. No, it's not because they are; it's because someone who is religious is easier to keep under control. Why do you think black people have all these churches and can open them up whenever they want to? White folks know that religion, as Karl Marx once said, "is the opiate of the oppressed masses." White folks use that Christianity bullshit as an economic and oppressive tool; black people try to use it as a solution to their problems and concerns. Let me put it to you like this: pray in one hand and shit in the other one and see which one fills up first.

White people, as a collective, as so predictably petty, no matter what they say or do. That is because in one way or form or another, their racist tendencies and values will come to surface. The story continues:

> The Sheppertons were delighted with him. He had come there looking for work just a month or two before, and modestly represented his qualifications. He had, he said, only recently received his discharge from the Army and was eager to get employment, at no matter what wage. He could cook he could tend the furnace, he knew how to drive a car – in fact, it seemed to us boys that there was very little that Dick Prosser could not do ...

All the things that white people want to relegate or confine black men to doing, it seemed that Prosser fit the bill. And as long as he was self-effacing and humble, that made him all the more desirable. If a peckerwood came across a white man with these traits, they would ridicule him, call him a "sissie" and harass him for days. But for a black man who be seen as someone who went to the army and served white interests, then was honorable discharged from said army, and then looked for work "no matter what wage"? He was the ideal "nigger" in the eyes of these white folks, both young and old. That means that they controlled him in the same way that Southern crackers controlled black people through sharecropping following enslavement.

Now we come to a key point. While acknowledging that there was "very little that Dick Prosser could not do," there was one thing that stood out in the minds of those white kids:

> He could certainly shoot. He gave a modest demonstration of his prowess one afternoon, with randy's .22, that left us gasping. He just lifted that little rifle in his powerful black hands as if it were a toy, without seeing to take aim, pointed it toward a strip of tin on which he had crudely marked out some bull's-eye circles, and he simply peppered the center of the bull's eye, putting twelve holes through a space one inch square, so fast that we could not even count the shots.

This is what surprises me: a black man being allowed to shoot a gun in front of some white boys? For one thing, it is surprising that their parents didn't find out and lynch Prosser right then and there. Secondly, why would Prosser show off his abilities to these white boys, knowing that there was a good chance that they might snitch? If a white man has a boy or his son run up to him and say, "Gollee, dad, that nigger sure knows how to shoot a gun!" do you know how fast it would take for that white man to round up a posse and come after that black man, I don't care how "humble" or "accommodating" he claims and seeks to be! I think Thomas Wolfe over-estimated the white kids' ability to keep a secret and he also assumed that Prosser was so dumb that he would do something this stupid.

That was one fuckup by Wolfe. But then, he talks about the boxing skills of Prosser as well:

> He knew how to box, too. I think he had been a regimental champion. At any rate, he was as cunning and crafty as a cat. He never boxed with us, of course, but Randy had two sets of gloves, and Dick used to coach us while we sparred. There was something amazingly tender and watchful about him. He taught us many things – how to lead, to hook, to counter and to block – but he was careful to see that we did not hurt each other.

So Prosser handled these white kids with care and, in violation of reality, they didn't run home and tell their parents. They didn't run home and use their skills that they had learned on their younger siblings. Again, this is not what would have taken place in the world of reality. But in the white world, even white kids have high moral values, a totally contradiction to the way it is in real life. They are the reasons for juvenile halls, school suspensions and expulsions and so on. White kids have always grown up to be just like their parents. And if their parents feel a certain way about black people, then it stands to reason that racism will be handed down from one generation to the next.

The story continues:

> He knew about football, too, and today he paused, a powerful, respectable-looking Negro man of thirty years or more, and watched us for a moment as we played. Randy took the ball and went up to him. "How do you hold it, Dick?" he said. "Is this right?"

Just like their ancestors and parents did: when in doubt, ask the black man and then after you learn, pretend as if you knew it all along. Even to this day if they want to learn the latest urban jargon, the latest fashions or anything that has to do with life in general, they ask us. Black kids taught white kids how to iron their clothes once they got to college; for a while, white boys on college campuses wouldn't iron their jeans. When they got black roommates and/or saw black kids doing it, that's when they caught on. Even in slavery we had to teach their women how to cook certain things and about how to suckle babies. We taught them agriculture and farming. As the poem by the Last Poets teaches, "How earnest you seemed/How well you did learn/How vile the reward I received in return."

The football tips from the black man to the white boys continue:

> Dick watched him attentively as he gripped the ball, and held it back over his shoulder. The Negro nodded approvingly and said, "That's right, Cap'n Shepperton. You've got it. Only," he said gently and now took the ball in his own powerful hand, "when you get a little oldah, yo' handses gits biggah and you gits a bettah grip."

Prosser was treating these kids the way that their fathers should have been treating them. And these kids appreciated it. After all, they knew that Prosser was no threat to them or their families, and while they might have had gratitude toward what he did, they also knew that he was one of those people that were known by their parents as "niggers." Therefore, as the Judge Roger Taney's ruling in the Dred Scott decision of 1957 made clear, "a black man has no rights that a white man is bound to respect."

Moving on:

> His own great hand, in fact, seemed to hold the ball as easily as if it were an apple. And holding it so a moment, he brought it back,

> aimed over his outstretched left and as if he were pointing a gun,
> and rifled it in a beautiful, whizzing spiral thirty yards or more to
> Gus. He then showed us how to kick, how to get the ball off the toe
> in such a way that it would rise and spiral cleanly. He knew how to
> do this, too. He must have got off kicks there, in the yard at the
> Sheppertons', that traveled fifty yards.

Once again the references to large hands. Thomas Wolfe, the author, had the same racial hang-ups, the same concerns about black physicality, as any other white man. They just couldn't believe the "size" of a lot of the physical characteristics of black men. Their pseudo-scientists tried to say that we were apes, that we had black sperm, that the cranial capacity of our skulls made us prone to criminality and all those theories – just to deal with the differences between black men and white men. And in white culture anything "different" is automatically viewed as being "deficient," with whiteness being the paragon and pinnacle of all that is human.

This incident must have been what it must have been like when the late, great Paul Robeson invented the forward pass in college football. This must have been what it was like as slowly but surely, black quarterbacks like Jefferson Street Joe Gilliam started beating out the likes of Terry Bradshaw and going up to Canada and winning Grey Cup titles like Warren Moon did. Big hands combined with speed; while they were claiming that the role of the quarterback was to stand in the pocket and deliver the ball (which they still do to this day), the black man was modifying (read: improving) the game by becoming a "dual threat." And today, that is becoming the norm. The white man saw it long ago, but he couldn't do it – so he outlawed it.

He did the same thing in basketball. He couldn't leap worth a shit and could only dunk if he was seven feet tall. But brothers who were six feet tall were swatting shots and dunking and to this day the white man seeks to simulate that leaping with trampolines and half-time tricks. When black men dunked at will they changed the rules of the game to stop Kareem, Abdul Jabbar (then Lew Alcindor) and to lesser extent, Wilt "the Stilt" Chamberlain. If they can't do it they find a way to outlaw it – until they can later find a way to market it so that they reap the lion's share of the profits.

Back to the story. Prosser taught the young white boys many things:

> He showed us how to make a fire, how to pile the kindling so that
> the flames shot up cone-wise, cleanly, without smoke or waste. He
> showed us how to strike a match with the thumbnail of one hand
> and keep and hold the flame in the strongest wind. He showed us
> how to lift a weight, how to tote a burden n our shoulders in the
> easiest way. There was nothing that he did not know. We were also

proud of him. Mr. Shepperton himself declared that Dick was the best man he'd ever had, the smartest darkey that he'd ever known.

All those skills and yet the assessment of Prosser was that he was the "smartest darkey" that this white man, Shepperton, had ever had. Instead of saying "ever had," what Wolfe should have said was "ever owned." Shepperton, like the boys doing all the complimenting, felt that Prosser was *their nigger* and as such, he was there to show and teach and serve *them.* Prosser was not even considered or judged in terms of being a human being, but he was top among the "darkeys." This is vintage white thinking and there is no doubt in my mind that it was also a reflection of the thinking of writer Thomas Wolfe.

But because of all these skills, there was always a kind of suspicion of Prosser because, after all, he was a black man. Check it out:

> And yet? He went too softly, at too swift a pace. He was there upon you sometimes like a cat. Looking before us, sometimes, seeing nothing buy the world before us, suddenly we felt a shadow at our backs and, looking up, would find that Dick was there. And there was something moving in the night. We never saw him come or go. Sometimes we would waken, startled and feel that we had heard a board creak, the soft clicking of a latch, a shadow passing swiftly. All was still.

This is the perpetuation of the "sneaky black" stereotype. These white people had the same stereotype when it came to Native Americans: "he walks like an Indian." Why would they do that? I believe it is because white men were so inept that they couldn't pay attention, so racist that their fear kept them from being cognizant of what was going on around them. So rather than attribute any "surprise attacks" to their own buffoonish neglect, it is a lot easier to make up this myth of people of color being "sneaky."

How else to explain why these kids would draw such superficial conclusions? Did they think that Dick feared them? Of course not. But like most white people you have to be fearful of that which you do not understand; in a word, assume the very worst about anyone who does not have white skin. That is how stereotypes such as these persist.

Now, check out Wolfe's version of black dialect:

> "Young white fokes, oh, young white gent'mun," – is soft voice ending in a moan, a kind f rhythm in his hips – "Oh, young white fokes, Ise tellin' *you"* – that soft low moan again – "You gotta love each othah like a brotha." He was deeply religious and went to church three times a week. He read his Bible every night. It was the only object on his square board table.

Religion is the one thing that assures the white man of controlling the masses of black people, not only here in the United States, but all over the world. It is the Christian religion that has black people praying in public and relying on "Jesus" to "take care of it" that keeps black people unilaterally and dictatorially at the bottom of this system. In *The Autobiography of Malcolm X*, Malcolm made the point in describing the effects of the Christian religion upon black people in this country:

> "The greatest miracle Christianity has achieved in America is that the black man in white Christian hands has not grown violent. It is a miracle that 22 million black people have not risen up against their oppressors – in which they would have been justified by all moral criteria, and even by the democratic tradition! It is a miracle that a nation of black people has so fervently continued to believe in a turn-the-other-cheek and heaven-for-you-after-you-die philosophy! It is a miracle that the American black people have remained a peaceful people, while catching all the centuries of hell that they have caught, here in white man's heaven!"

The short story, "The Chlld by Tiger" was first published in 1937. And yet you can see the emphasis that the writer, Thomas Wolfe, placed on the level of religious commitment that Dick Prosser displayed and practiced. Since I have established that this white man knows so little about black values, culture and life, why would he continue to drive home the point about religion and the Bible? I'll tell you why: because at this point he is painting a picture of how he – and most white people – view "the perfect nigger." It is a black person who is humble, subservient to a fault, and filled with "de holy spirit." These three characteristic combine to create a being that can be totally controlled by any white person – man, woman or child.

Recall Malcolm X's words before we move on: "! It is a miracle that the American black people have remained a peaceful people, while catching all the centuries of hell that they have caught, here in white man's heaven!" And this is something that Thomas Wolfe would have considered had he been able to view black people as human beings; had he respected black people as individuals who want to be free just as the white man boasts of his freedom. If he had considered the fact that by writing that Prosser was a former war veteran that he (Prosser) might have thought about fighting for the rights of Americans and then returning home to legal segregation, racism and discrimination. But he is quick to point home, in a regular basis, the "religious" orientation of Prosser. This is not by accident.

The story continues:

> Sometimes Dick would come out of his little basement room, and
> his eyes would be red, as if he had been weeping. We would know,
> then, that he had been reading his Bible. There would be times
> when he would almost moan when he talked to us, a kind of
> hymnal chant that came from some deep and fathomless
> intoxication of the spirit, and that transported him.

And this, dear reader, is how white boys like Thomas Wolfe view religion and those who truly believe. They see it as something to be gawked at, and they view people who talk about it as being somehow "possessed." And check out how they also view the people who are faith believers:

> For us, it was a troubling and bewildering experience. We tried to
> laugh it off and make jokes about it. But there was something in it
> so dark and strange and full of feeling that we could not fathom
> that our jokes were hollow, and the trouble in our minds and in or
> hearts remained.

Making fun of an adult black man who they claim to have all this admiration and respect for? This is not a contradiction you might presume it to be. To far too many white folks – including white children – black people nothing more than comic relief. What they read about, what they hear in schools and later on, what they see on television and at the movies, all drive home the point that no matter how serious an issue is in black life, somewhere a joke or a goof can and will be found. How else to explain how something that the boys viewed as "bewildering" nevertheless culminate with laughs and jokes? At the root of it is the belief that any black endeavor or activity is not worthy of being taken seriously.

Today, in 2016 I am sure that white folks act in a similar way when they hear black preachers, witness black "prayer vigils" and hear all those gospel hymns coming from a people who are impoverished and ghettoized. Remember the Malcolm X quote from earlier where Malcolm said, in part, "It is a miracle that the American black people have remained a peaceful people, while catching all the centuries of hell that they have caught, here in white man's heaven!" The white man spends trillions on leisure and top-notch necessities enjoying a heaven right here on earth, perhaps recognizing the value in the title of the old Ohio Players cut, "Heaven Must Be Like This." When he hears about or witnesses us praying and talking about "faith" and "hope," and claiming that "Jesus will handle it," his reaction is undoubtedly similar to that of the boys had to Prosser's religiosity.

More evidence of this allegation follows:

> Sometimes on these occasions his speech would be made up of
> some weird jargon of Biblical phrases, of which he seemed to have
> hundreds, and which he wove together in this strange pattern of his
> emotion in a sequence that was meaningless to us, but to which he
> himself had the coherent clue. "Oh, young white fokes," he would
> begin, moaning gently, "de dry bones in de valley. I tell you, white
> fokes de day is comin' when He's comin' on dis earth again to sit
> in judgment. He'll put the sheep upon de right hand and de goats
> upon de left. Oh, white fokes, white fokes, de Armageddon day's a
> comin', white fokes, an de dry bones in de valley."

"Weird jargon of Biblical phrases"? Wolfe, as the writer of this story and the creator of these characters knows the point he is trying to get across: he is poking fun at this black man and that man's devotion to the Bible. If the "jargon" was "weird," why didn't the youth ask Prosser about it? From that is written above it seems that Prosser was trying tell those white boys that their race had an ass whipping coming. Why else would he be telling them about Armageddon, which is basically the "end of days"? This would not be the first time in their history that white people had ignored the writing on the wall and ended up paying for it. But let me not get ahead of myself. The story and the racist leanings of the author (and hence, his characters) continues:

> Or again, we could hear him singing as he went about his work, in
> his deep rich voice, so full of warmth and strength, so full of
> Africa, singing hymns that were not only of his own race but
> familiar to us all. I don't know where he learned them. Perhaps
> they were remembered from his Army days. Perhaps he had
> learned them in the service of former masters …

So full of Africa? Hymns that are of his own race, "but familiar to us all"? Such bullshit! Something can be familiar to you and you can still disrespect or hate it. What do these white assholes or the author know about Africa? Africa is a continent, not a fuckin' country or a city. There is as much diversity in Africa as there is anywhere else Africans don't sing those fuckin' slave hymns! Those brothers and sisters in bondage were singing about getting the fuck away from whitey! But the white man was so stupid, he couldn't interpret the coded messages! But rather than admit as much, the peckerwoods attribute the talents and tenor of Prosser to the Army days. But the ultimate insult is yet to come.

It is written that, "Perhaps he had learned them in the service of former masters." What former masters? Prosser wasn't born in bondage! This is 1937, and formal enslavement had ended over 70 years prior! Of what "former masters" is this peckerwood speaking? So what do we have? We have (1) the glorification of that which is white, and (2) the consequent debasement of Africa, Prosser's religious beliefs and his expression of those beliefs. Remember this, because when Prosser starts bustin' caps, you'll understand why.

Moving right along:

> He drove the Sheppertons to church on Sunday morning, and would wait for them throughout the morning service. He would come up to the side door of the church while the service was going on, neatly dressed in his good dark suit, holding his chauffer's hat respectfully in his hand, and stand there humbly and listen during the course of the entire sermon.

To far too many white folks, Prosser is the prototype "negro." Waiting patiently; literally "driving Miss Daisy;" neatly dressed; and we can't forget his "standing there humbly and listening." Any white man in this situation would be considered an "under-achiever," but then again, a white man would not have had to stand outside of the church. Remember: the church is supposed to be a house of the Lord. So since these churches had a "no niggas allowed" policy, guess who that makes "the lord" of that church? The white man,that's who. His religion reflects his views, values, aims and intentions

As evidence that the white man views religion as nothing more than an extension of his own power, check out the following:

> And then, when the hymns were sung, and the great rich sound would swell and roll out into the quiet air of Sunday, Dick would stand and listen, and sometimes he would join in quietly in the song. A number of these favorite Presbyterian hymns we heard him singing many times in a low rich voice as he went about his work around the house. He would sing "Who Follows in His Train?" or "Alexander's Glory Song," or "Rock of Ages," or "Onward, Christian Soldiers!"

These boys homoerotically watched Prosser's every move, or so it appears. But then again, isn't that what American society in the year 2016 does? Whether it's the welfare system, the cops, the FBI, fashion designers, landlords – some peckerwood is always staring at us, checking out what we're doing, longing to write news stories or file a report. They long to be like us without actually having to go what we have to go through: police ass whippings, discriminatory treatment and the kind of shit that is described in the following excerpt:

> And yet? Well, nothing happened – there was just "a flying hint from here and there," and the sense of something passing in the night. Turning into the square one day as Dick was driving Mr.

Shepperton to town, Lon Everett skidded murderously around the corner, sideswiped Dick, and took the fender off. The Negro was out of the car like a cat and got his master out. Shepperton was unhurt …

A car accident and Prosser seems to care more about Shepperton than he does for himself. This is what Malcolm X was talking about in his description of the" house negro" during enslavement. In his classic, "Message to the Grass Roots," Malcolm articulated the following:

> To understand this, you have to go back to what [the] young brother here referred to as the house Negro and the field Negro -- back during slavery. There was two kinds of slaves. There was the house Negro and the field Negro. The house Negroes - they lived in the house with master, they dressed pretty good, they ate good 'cause they ate his food -- what he left. They lived in the attic or the basement, but still they lived near the master; and they loved their master more than the master loved himself. They would give their life to save the master's house quicker than the master would. The house Negro, if the master said, "We got a good house here," the house Negro would say, "Yeah, we got a good house here." Whenever the master said "we," he said "we." That's how you can tell a house Negro.

And did Prosser not live in Shepperton's basement? And in this case, did Prosser not act like the house negro when it is described that such a person," would give their life to save the master's house quicker than the master would"? Now that Shepperton is unhurt, check out other reactions from Prosser:

> Lon Everett climbed out and reeled across the street, drunk as a sot at three o'clock. He swung viciously, clumsily, at the Negro, smashing him in the face. Blood trickled down from the flat black nostrils and from the thick liver-colored lips. Dick did not move. But suddenly the whites of his eyes were shot with red, his bleeding lips bared for a moment over the white ivory of his teeth. Lon smashed at him again. The Negro took it full in the face again; his hands twitched slightly, but he did not move. They collared the drunken sot and hauled him off and locked him up. Dick stood there for a moment; then he wiped his face and turned to see what damage had been done to the car. No more now, but there were those who saw it who remembered later how the eyes went red.

Taking an ass whipping from an inferior opponent. Can you believe that there was an entire culture of behavior that promoted such race-based behavior? That's why when segregation was lifted and civil rights laws passed, we got to kicking peckerwoods in the ass every chance we got. And it's still going on today so much to the point that unlike the "take it and like it" behavior they imposed on our grandparents and ancestors, these pale muthafuckas play the role of "victim" every chance they get. Our kids are kicking them in the ass, including the cops. But such behavior as a history. Study and you'll see this behavior is a clear-cut example of the principle of the boomerang.

But poor Prosser was trapped in a different time. Read again where, "Dick stood there for a moment; then he wiped his face and turned to see what damage had been done to the car. No more now, but there were those who saw it who remembered later how the eyes went red." Putting the condition of the car above his own well-being. But when those eyes went red, that was a warning sign. In the words from the old TV show "Lost in Space," "Danger Will Robinson, danger!"

The story then introduces another black person, a sistah:

> Another thing: the Sheppertons had a cook named Pansy Harris. She was a comely Negro wench, young, plump, black as the ace of spaces, a good-hearted girl with a deep dimple in her cheeks and faultless teeth, bared in a most engaging smile. No one ever saw Dick speak to her. No one ever saw her glance at him, or him at her, and yet that smilingly good-natured wench became as mournful-silent as silent-sullen as midnight pitch. She went about her work as mournfully as if she were going to a funeral. The gloom deepened all about her. She answered sullenly now when spoken to.

Let's analyze the preceding paragraph for the racist imagery and implications, of which I shall address four of them.

First, the name "Pansy Harris." The author of this story if Thomas Wolfe, one of the most accomplished and prolific writers of his generation. But this just goes to show, once again, that you can have a great skill and still be dead wrong when you start writing about things that you don't have a clue about. In the case of Thomas Wolfe, I would say that he was a total idiot when it comes to issues of race and black history. As a result, of all the names he could have selected for this woman, he names her "Pansy." Why? I'll tell you why: because it's a nominal stereotyped name. Akin to "Hattie," Sha-Nay-Nay, "Butterfly," "Daniqua" and so many more, when you hear names like this you know that the person with that name has got to be black.

Secondly, the description of Pansy being "a comely Negro wench" who as "black as the ace of spades." This is Wolfe's way of saying that she was nice looking "for a nigga gal." And why did she have to be a "wench"? Why are the surroundings and other people, even the derelicts, described in human terms, but when it comes to black people we find and encounter all these stereotypes and veiled insults? You know why: Wolfe is a racist muthafucka, that's why.

Third, the claim that "no one ever saw Dick speak to her." What the writer means to say is that nobody "white" ever saw them conversing. And that's the way it is in reality, then and now: if a white man didn't see it, it couldn't have taken place. This is the way it is in a racially segregated context. They must have communicated because as you will find out later, Prosser was fucking her! But this is a good time to show how white novelists think and how they characters they create reflect the views and values of the writer.

Fourth and finally, Pansy going about her work "mournful – silent as silent …" As compared to what? This is that old "whistle while you work" bullshit that the white man tried to use to paint black enslaved persons as exhibiting; they worker who sang out of pure ecstasy. The farmhand who whistled while he lifted bales of cotton. In that way, they (the slave masters) could dupe themselves into thinking they were doing niggas a favor by enslaving them and not have to deal with the fact that they (slave masters) were some sick, perverted, brutal white muthafuckas.

Let us move on with the story:

> One night toward Christmas she announced that she was leaving. In response to all entreaties, all efforts to find the reason for her sudden and unreasonable decision, she had no answer except a sullen repetition of the assertion that she had to leave. Repeated questionings did finally wring from her a sudden statement that her husband needed her at home. More than this she would not say, and even this excuse was highly suspect, because her husband was a Pullman porter, only home two days a week and well accustomed to do himself such housekeeping tasks as she might do for him.

What you just read is an example of white arrogance and paternalism. The woman wants to leave and the automatic assumption is that her decision is "unreasonable and sudden." White people are so full of themselves that they think that working for them is a fuckin' walk in the park. They think that the black servant, butler, chauffeur, shine boy or whatever should simply be ecstatic to have a white "boss" or "supervisor." All they have to do is look at two sets of statistics of today, a reflection of their history, to show that they are not liked, even by their own people: (1) the sky high divorce rate and (2) the concept of "TGIF" – Thank God It's Friday" – another way of saying, "I can't wait to get away from this fuckin' white workplace." This is white-on-white "hate" that is never addressed because if it were, the entire white system would break down.

Moreover, if they knew that Pansie's husband had a job as a Pullman porter, then why couldn't her decision be based on the fact that his income was enough to support the two of them and therefore, she was in a position to leave the job? Instead, these white folks turn the decision into an antagonistic one by treating Pansie as some kind of "uppity" black:

> The Sheppertons were fond of her. They tried to find the reason for her leaving. Was she dissatisfied? "No'm – an implacable monosyllable, mournful, unrevealing as the night. Had she been offered a better job elsewhere? "No'm' – as untelling as before. If they offered her more wages, would she stay with them? "No'm," again and again, sullen and unyielding until finally the exasperated mistress threw up her hands in a gesture of defeat and said. "All right, then, Pansy. Have it your own way, if that's the way you feel. Only for heaven's sake don't leave us in the lurch until we get another cook."

Even when defeated and dealt with, white people still have to feel like they've had the last word. Ms. Shepperton tells the woman, "All right, then, Pansy. Have it your own way, if that's the way you feel." Pansy already had it her way, and let them know of her decision. But the cultural super-ego of white folks just won't accept a black person making a decision that does not include them. And to ensure that the white ego and status are not threatened by this "nigger," Ms. Shepperton makes both a demand and appeal that, "Only for heaven's sake don't leave us in the lurch until we get another cook."

Do you see what she's done? She's flipped the power relationship from being told what black woman has decided to do to making it appear as if the decision that was made is somehow an affront to white family life. Leaving them in the lurch? I have an idea: why not get up off your white flat ass and perform some of your own household-related tasks? White folks are so lazy they would rather wait around to find someone else to do their work than to do a little work on their own. The idea of having a "maid," a "butler," a "chauffeur" and/or a "servant" is a status symbol, even to those living on the fringes of the lower middle class.

And check out the following description by the author Wolfe:

> This, at length, with obvious reluctance, the girl agreed to. Then, putting on her hat and coat and taking her bag of "leavings" she was allowed to take home with her at night, she went out the kitchen door and made her sullen and morose departure.

Referring to a grown woman as "the girl"? Again, this thinking hails back to the days of enslavement when grown black men were "boys" and full grown black women, like Pansy, were "girls." He knows that black people referred to "leavings" which was what we today call "leftovers" – the stuff white people didn't eat or want. Sometimes the white folks would use some of those "leavings" as a part of the salary in lieu of monetary payment. Black people, being powerless, couldn't say anything about it.

Wolfe says that Pansy made "a sullen and morose departure." What would the purpose be in describing Pansy in such down and out and ill-mood-related terms? The fact is she had something more important on her mind and had to get on with her life. How does that relate to these white folks in a city that is segregated and where they normally don't even give "Niggertown" an afterthought? In the same way that negative descriptors are used to describe Prosser, so too it is with Pansy. And the common denominator in providing these racist in presumptive adjectives.

Continuing on with the story:

> This was Saturday night, a little after eight o'clock. That afternoon Randy and I had been fooling around the basement and, seeing that Dick's door was slightly ajar, we looked in to see if he was there. The little room was empty, swept and spotless, as it had always been.

Earlier in this analysis I made a reference to the case of Scott v. Sanford of 1857 (also known as "the Dred Scott case"). I recall sharing with you the findings of the Justice Taney who ruled that, "a black man has no rights that a white man is bound to respect." What you just read in the aforementioned excerpt is but one more example of it. Even white boys feel that they have some kind of "right" to peer into the room of a grown man and make value judgments about that man's life. And lo and behold, check out what took place:

> But we didn't notice that! We saw it! At the same moment, our breaths caught sharply in a gasp of startled wonderment. Randy was the first to speak. "Look!" he whispered. "Do you see it?" See it! My eyes were glued upon it. Squarely across the bare board table, blue-dull, deadly in its murderous efficiency, lay a modern repeating rifle. Beside it lay a box containing one hundred rounds of ammunition, and behind it, surely in the center, face downward on the table, was the familiar cover of Dick's worn old Bible.

Translation: "a nigger with a gun!" Even the young whites knew that this was something to fear. After all those years of enslaving their people and keeping them out of school, banning them from public accommodations, lynching and gunning down the men and raping the women, the last thing that a white man wants to see is, what the title of the Robert F. Williams denotes, "Negroes With Guns." That's why the Black Panthers, the Revolutionary Action Movement and so other 1960s "radical groups" scared whitey so. Oh, he talks a great game and on his movies and TV shows he can handle anything with "lone wolf" bravado. But in real life, he's a coward with an attitude, a bully who has to have his mob buddies and his military standing behind him as he continues to sell woof tickets to the world.

But again, a black man has no rights a white man is bound to respect, not even young white boys. They are the ones violating Prosser's privacy, but let the story tell it, the black man has somehow done something to them by just having a rifle in his own room!

The master-slave tradition kicks in from a socio-psychological perspective, as the following paragraph points out:

> Then he was on us like a cat. He was there like a great dark
> shadow before we knew it. We turned, terrified. He was there
> above us, his thick lips bared above his gums, his eyes gone small
> and red as rodents'. "Dick!" Randy gasped, and moistened his dry
> lips. "Dick!" he fairly cried now. It was all over like a flash. Dick's
> mouth closed. We could see the whites of his eyes again. He
> smiled and said softly, affably, "Yes, suh, Cap'n Shepperton. Yes,
> suh! You gent'mun lookin' at my rifle?" he said, and moved into
> the room.

Look at the combination of what I call "beastification references" that are then combined with color coded and racist descriptors: "on us like a cat," "great dark shadow," "thick lips bared," "eyes gone small and red as rodents.' Remember the quality of Wolfe's writing and the purpose of a good novelist or storyteller is to paint images in the minds of the readers. What image could Wolfe be trying to project other than to paint Prosser as part animal, part savage? And since Prosser can immediately become a nice and affable guy right after that, the general image is one of Prosser being a black Jekyll-and-Hyde and the belief that "all blacks are savages underneath" is therefore justified.

But remember these are young boys, but they are white; so they are protected and defended by white privilege and a racist system. Therefore, look at the reaction that Wolfe provides:

> I gulped and nodded my head and couldn't say a word, and Randy
> whispered, "Yes." And both of us still stared at him, with an
> expression of appalled and fascinated interest.

But take notice that none of their actions was one of "fear." This huge man who they describe as being just short of a beast, these young white boys get caught violating his personal living space, and they nevertheless have the unmitigated gall to be "appalled and fascinated" with interest? What is this – the zoo? Who do they see Prosser as: an educated gorilla? What kind of white supremacist shit is this? They are in the wrong and yet the stand there continuing to be in judgment of a man who is twice their age.

More of Wolfe's version of black dialect can be found in the following passage:

> Dick shook his head and chuckled. "Can't do without my rifle, white fokes. No, suh!" he shook his head good-naturedly again. "Ole Dick, he's – he's – he's an old Ahmy man, you know. If they take my rifle away from him why, that's just like takin' candy from a little baby. Yes, suh!" he chuckled, and picked the weapon up affectionately. "Old Dick felt Christmas comin' on –he – he – I reckon he must have felt it in his bone" – he chuckled – "So I been savin' up my money. I just thought I'd hide this heah and keep it as a big supprise fo' the young white fokes untwil Christmas morning. Then I was going' to take the young white fokes out and show 'em how to shoot."

Playing the role of the coon tricks white people every time because that is what they think we are. They got outsmarted thousands of times during enslavement as there were more than 1,500 recorded slave insurrections. That means two things: if these were the numbers that made the papers, then that means it must have been three or four times that many. And secondly, in order for these black people to "overthrow" those white folks, it took courage and planning. It took a cultural commitment. It was not like that "way down upon de Swanee Ribber" bullshit that they keep imposing on our children when they discuss slavery. It was about brains, outwitting that white boy, knowing his tendencies and then taking advantage of it. That is what you see and hear from Prosser in the preceding excerpt.

And another thing you see is the appeal to the white ego. If you can bamboozle the white man into thinking that he's more than he really is – and that's not difficult – then you can get him to at least temporarily relax his defenses. Christmas is the white man's holiday, the day when they look forward to making tons of money and unifying with their fellow racists and families. And that is when he is at his weakest.

The words from Prosser appear to have worked, but the strategy continues:

> We had begun to breathe more easily now, and almost as if we'd
> been under the spell of the Pied Piper of Hamelin, we had followed
> him, step by step into the room.

This is the same type of spell that black men put on white women to this very day. How else to explain a class of women who have white privilege working for them being willing to give it all up just for someone who says the right thing and then plows them with black dick? We call it our "rap," but black men use it all the time to get over on white people by playing into their racist stereotypical beliefs. For instance, the "myth of de po' black family." Result: food stamps, section 8 housing and utility assistance. How about "the myth of the po' single mutha"? Result: more government programs (read: reparations) and the relaxing of white defenses. How about: "the myth of the dumb black man." Result: relaxed tendencies, the sharing of secrets and the belief that they (whites) have everything under control.

We shall see what we shall see. Remember that the Pied Piper of Hamlin saved the town by leading all the "rats" into the river to drown. At the time the people believed that the rats were the reason for the plague so in doing what he did, the Pied Piper saved the entire town. In like manner, black people who have the guts can save their neighborhoods and communities by leading the good-meaning white racists out. And Prosser, through his actions later in the story, sent a message of white folks that black people had better be respected. More on this later.

The story continues:

> "Yes, suh," Dick chuckled. "I was just fixin' to hide this gun away
> twill Chritmas Day, but Cap'n Shepperton – hee!" He chuckled
> heartily and slapped his thigh. "You can't fool ole Cap'n
> Shepperton. He just must've smelled this le gun right out. He
> comes right in and sees it befo' I has a chance to tu'n around ...
> Now, white folkes" – Dick's voice fell to a tone of low and
> winning confidence – "now that you've found out, I'll tell you
> what I'll do. If you'll just keep it a supprise from the other white
> fokes twill Christmas Day, I'll take all you gent'mun out and let
> you shoot it. Now, cose," he went on quietly, with a shade of
> resignation, "If you want to tell on me, you can, but" – here his
> voice fell again, with just the faintest yet most eloquent shade of
> sorrowful regret – "old dick was lookin' fahwad to this; hopin' to
> give all the white fokes a supprise Christmas Day."

One way you can appeal to any white person is to ask them to keep a secret and if they do, they'll get a big fat reward. They are the ones who created the concept of the wanted poster, which at one time included the statement, "Wanted: Dead or Alive," remember. Bring or give us what we want and we'll give you a big ol' surprise at the end. We don't care how you get it, just bring it to us. And that is how these young boys were thinking: "Gee minitly, we get to shoot a gun and all we have to do is not tell our parents. What a great deal!" And they figuratively took that pledge all the way to the bank.

The blood bank.

> We promised earnestly that we would keep his secret as if it were our own. We fairly whispered our solemn vow. We tiptoed away our of the little basement room as if we were afraid our very footsteps might betray the partner of our confidence. This was four o'clock on Saturday afternoon. Already, there was a somber moaning of the wind, gray storm clouds sweeping over. The threat of snow was in the air.

What appears to be innocent white kids is betrayed by the way that the environment and the conditions are described: somber moaning of the wind," "gray storms," "threat of snow" in the air. It's as if the author is implying that a supreme force was somehow involved in the lives of these people and in doing so, also insinuates that the white man and his life decisions are on par with the actions of God. That is why the white man has historically and accurately been accused of having a "god complex."

The negativity is described by the writer, as if the peace and tranquility of white life was somehow about to experience an "attack" by some "black force," as they are prone to say when something bad is about to happen. Check it out:

> Snow fell that night. It came howling down across the hills. It swept in on us from the Smokies. By seven o'clock the air was blind with sweeping snow, the earth was carpeted, the streets were numb. The storm howled on, around houses warm with crackling fires and shaded light. All life seemed to have withdrawn into thrilling isolation. A horse went by upon the street with muffled hoofs. Storm shook the houses. The world was numb. I went to sleep upon this mystery, lying in the darkness, listening to that exultancy of storm, to that dumb wonder, that enormous and attentive quietness of snow, with something dark and jubilant in my soul I could not utter.

What is described above can best be described as a "quaint scenario." All is at peace and the snow is muffling the sounds of horse hoofs. Even if there were cars, the sounds of the tires would have a strange sound of being quieted by snow. I was born and raised in snowy terrains so I can relate to the conditions being described by Wolfe. But as is the case with most white writers, such scenarios are used to set up something dire, something sinister that is about to take place. In that way, once hell break loose they can do what they normally do: blame it on the niggas.

Here we go:

> A little after one o'clock that morning I was awakened by the ringing of a bell. It was the fire bell of the city hall, and it was beating an alarm – a hard fast stroke that I had never heard before. Bronze with peril. Clangorous through the snow-numbed silence of the air, it had a quality of instancy and menace I had never known before. I leaped up and ran to the window to look for the telltale glow against the sky. But almost before I looked, those deadly strokes beat in upon my brain the message that this was no alarm for fire. It w as a savage clangorous alarm to the whole town, a brazen tongue to warn mankind against the menace of some peril, secret, dark, and unknown, greater than fire or flood could ever be.

Notice the way this white bastards stirs the kettle of white racism. Look at all of these inflammatory terms used to instill fear in the reader: "clangorous," "instancy and menace," "deadly strokes," "savage clangorous alarm," "brazen tongue," "menace of some peril," "secret, dark and unknown." With descriptors such as these, the reader cannot help but fear and hate whatever the source of all this commotion and rancor is.

In response to the macabre description offered above,

> I got instantly, in the most overwhelming and electric way, the sense that the whole town had come to life. All u and down the street the houses were beginning to light up. Next door, the Shepperton house was ablaze with light from top to bottom. Even as I looked, Mr. Shepperton, wearing an overcoat over his pajamas, ran down the snow-covered steps and padded out across the snow-covered walk toward the street. People were beginning to run out of doors. I heard excited shouts and questions everywhere. I saw Nebraska Crane come pounding down the middle of the street. I knew that he as coming for me and Randy ...

The fear is beginning to spread. The people who know what's going on can't wait to tell anyone who will listen. This is the beginning of what is called "contagion," where crowds of people begin to form and grow in response to something. More on that later. Let us continue with the community response:

> As he ran by Shepperton's, he put his fingers to his mouth and whistled piercingly. It was a signal we all knew. I was all ready by the time he came running down the alley toward our cottage. He hammered on the door; I was already there. "Come on!" he said,

> panting with excitement, his black eyes burning with an intensity
> I'd never seen before. "Come on!" he cried. We were half-way out
> across the yard by now. "It's that nigger. He's gone crazy and is
> running wild."

Three words that will send a chill up any peckerwood's back: "it's that nigger." This is second only to, "it's THOSE niggers." And of course, the final scream, at least in the South during enslavement, was "There goes that nigger – let's get him!" But better the former than the latter. Now, that we know the source of the fear and hysteria, let us discuss the concept of "contagion." You will see and better understand why white mob rule happens so frequent throughout American history and why in this story, the time was most apparent.

It begins with a study from crowd psychology. Le Bon (2002) attributed crowd behavior to the 'collective racial unconscious' of the mob overtaking individuals' sense of self and personality and personal responsibility. According to Le Bon, relieved of individual responsibility, individuals will behave in a more primal fashion. He asserts, 'by the mere fact that he forms part of an organized crowd, a man descends several rungs on the ladder of civilization.' A modern comparison might be the teenager who argues that his own actions of toilet papering the principal's house weren't so bad because everybody else was doing it, too. . (Le Bon, 2002).

Add to this the fact that the white people who turn into mobs and adopt a form of lynch law area also in agreement that they are "the good guys" and are dealing with "a problem," then you have a recipe for what is called "contagion." Contagion theory suggests that crowds exert a sort of hypnotic influence on their members. The hypnotic influence combined with the anonymity of belonging to a large group of people, even just for that moment, results in irrational, emotionally charged behavior. Or, as the name implies, the frenzy of the crowd is somehow contagious, like a disease, and the contagion feeds upon itself, growing with time. In the end, the crowd has assumed a life of its own, stirring up emotions and driving people toward irrational, even violent action. . (Le Bon, 2002).

And so it is with what I call the "get the nigger" syndrome. This is a part of what scholar Oliver C. Cox referred to as "the manhunt tradition." With this important information out of the way, you will now better understand what is about to happen in this, yet another "all-American town:"

> "Wh-wh-what nigger?" I gasped, pounding at his heels. Even
> before he spoke, I had the answer. Mr. Crane had already come out
> of his house buttoning his heavy policeman's overcoat as he came.
> He had paused to speak for a moment to Mr. Shepperton, and I
> heard Shepperton says quickly, in a low voice," Which way did he

go?" Then I heard somebody cry, "It's that nigger of
Shepperton's!"

"What nigger"? Muthafucka how many niggas do you know? He's not
talking about the ones that you read about or see on television! He's talking about
the one whose ass you been kissing and whose physical attributes you've been
homoerotically observing, that's who!

But it gets cleared up and we are informed that, "it's the nigger of
Shepperton's." Translation: it's the nigger who belongs to, is owned, and is the
responsibility of Sheppertons. Just like during enslavement: if you see a black man,
you know he is owned by someone white. This teaches us that although formal
enslavement has ended, the same slave master mentality and a similar master-slave
relationship continues to exist. There are more similarities as you are about to find
out:

> Mr. Shepperton turned and went quickly back across his yard
> toward the house. His wife and two girls stood huddled in the open
> doorway, white, trembling, holding themselves together, their arms
> thrust into the wide sleeves of their kimonos.

Yeah, now they tremble because their lily-white world is being threatened
by someone who is not white, someone who is willing to use the same violence
that the ancestors of these peckerwoods used to steal that land many decades
earlier. The same violence that Prosser was taught to use when he was in the army
is the violence these suburban white people fear most. Their history, as a
collective, is one of living in fear based on skin color. When they fight each other,
it is not as mobs but as formal military units with rules and protocols. It is when
they fight (or "attack") black people that their true savagery comes to the fore. You
are about to read evidence that substantiates this allegation.

Panic is spreading rapidly about the white community. Black people tend to
feel the same way black people feel when we see cops riding down on us, speeding
through our area with high speed chases. Shooting blindly in pursuit of a single
"suspect" and not giving a shit about collateral damage. In a word, the panic
continues to spread:

> The telephone in the Shepperton's house was ringing like mad, but
> no one was paying any attention to it. I heard Mrs. Shepperton say
> quickly, as he ran up the steps, "Is it Dick?" He nodded and passed
> her brusquely, gong toward the phone. At this moment Nebraska
> whistled piercingly again upon his fingers, and Randy Shepperton
> ran past his mother and down the steps. She called sharply to him.
> He paid no attention to her. When he came up, I saw that his fine

thin face was white as a sheet. He looked at me and whispered,
"It's Dick!" And in a moment, "They say he's killed four people."

At this point let me advance a theory of symbolic racism that I think permeates the mind of the writer, Thomas Wolfe, and of course of the characters that he has created in order to paint the picture of race relations that he decided to paint.

Now Richard Prosser, the black man who has been treated in a second class fashion, is known as "Dick," right. And of course, he is an African-American, right? And a commonly used term for a male penis is a "dick," right? So in other words, once he decides to go on his rampage, the fear of men and women alike is of "Black Dick." Are you with me?

I believe this is a metaphor for the fear of the black penis. And if you look at the way that the characters have acted in response to "black dick," there are definite parallels. There is no mention of the white female response to "black dick" before the riot episode takes place is there? And why should there be? There is a social rule that they are not supposed to be interested in black dick. Even though he lived in the basement of the house where a white woman resided with her husband and child, this is another metaphor for where a "black dick" should be placed. It should be bottled up, buttoned up and never exposed. Black Dick never really went anywhere and he was under the control of the people he worked for. When he drove them he was "covered up" in a suit and hat and programmed not to be "exposed" (read: erect). He was programmed, as is the black dick, to stay under control in public and when you're anywhere close to a white man or woman. It would entice and scare the latter and anger the former. This is how it has been throughout racial interactions in this country.

So when the "black Dick" becomes angered and busts out of his former persona of passivity, the entire town goes berserk. Every time he "shoots" (ejaculates) white people fall. When the brown sperm enters white society, because it is a dominant gene, it both phenotypically and genetically "eliminates" the white gene. That is why white women who get pregnant by men of color have brown, not white, babies. And what is why albinism is considered a kind of "disease," because it is the absence of color.

So the black Dick is ejaculating all over the insulated town (womb), and the white man must destroy it – just as he did during slavery whether he had a reason to do so or not. Every black man that was lynched was deemed a "threat" to the community on some level. A *genetic* threat. The black Dick must be segregated, isolated and kept under control and aware from the "white purity" of the white race. That is the only way to explain the white man's fear of the black male. Even to this day, you lock them up among their own, you isolate them in ghettos, you arrest them at the slightest provocation and when "allowed" on college campuses, you make sure that they are there as athletes and as such, have to follow special rules and protocols to keep them away from the white females (although this attempt fails because of the high slut-level of these white girls).

It's only a theory, but remember that increasing numbers of young black people understand this very well – as do white women. Many of them think a brown-skinned child is the cutest being on the planet and therefore crave to embrace them, either through pregnancy or adoption. But things were not as "liberated" back in 1937 as they are now, and the taboos continued to persist. Blacks could not even legally marry whites until the year 1970. Read the case of *Loving v. Virginia* and you can learn more about the real hang-ups of the white race.

The word "dick" is being shouted but it's a proper noun in this story. So the fear is of "Dick" Prosser. Now, let us move on and see how one innocent "dick" affects an entire town of people who, before he became erect (stood up for himself), and as long as he was bottled up in the "underwear" of the Shepperton basement, was overlooked and bypassed.

Moving on:

> "With –" I couldn't finish. Randy nodded dumbly, and we both stared there for a minute, are now of the murderous significance of the secret we had kept, with a sudden sense of guilt and fear, as if somehow the crime lay on our shoulders. Across the street a window banged up in the parlor of the Sugg's house, and Old Man Suggs appeared in the window, clad only in his nightgown, his brutal old face inflamed with excitement, his shock of silvery white hair awry, is powerful shoulders, and his thick hands gripping his crutches. "He's coming this way!" he bawled to the world in general. "They say he lit out across the square! He's headed out in this direction!"

The big black Dick is coming! These white people are reacting to this man the same way that their movies show them acting toward King Kong, Godzilla, Frankenstein's monster and other "creatures." No white man would be treated this way even if he did gun down other whites. It's all about race, Thomas Wolfe knew it, and he exploited it in this story. His miscalculations and errors on race relations notwithstanding, he has painted a picture of white historical violence against black people in general and both Dick and Pansy, in particular. These two characters represent what little Wolfe knows about the black male and the black female, respectively. They are personifications of the "nigger" and the "negress," to use white vernacular.

All this calamity and contagion leads to the following: "Mr. Crane paused to yell back impatiently over his shoulder, "No, he went down South Dean Street! He's heading for Wilton and the river! I've already heard from headquarters!" The word spreads like wildfire when the perceived and real danger has to do with a black man with a gun. It's not only that he has a gun; there's a subconscious understanding by these white folks that they are getting what they deserve. Just the fact that there is a "Niggertown" that is isolated and held in abeyance while they (whites) experience the fruits of American society (which those same "niggers" helped to build) is justification for anger and lashing out. That's why when it happens from time to time, white fear is of the highest order.

The story moves on:

> Automobiles were beginning to roar and sputter all along the
> street. Across the street I could hear Mr. Potterham sweating over
> his. He would whirl the crank a dozen times or more; the engine
> would catch for a moment, cough and putter, and then die again.
> Gus ran out-of-doors with a kettle of boiling water and began to
> pour it feverishly down the radiator spout.

These peckerwoods were serious! They were out there in snow, cranking up their raggedy ass cars, fetching rifles, running around like chickens with their heads cut off, just because a black man – one whom they had ignored and dogged for years – was gunning down some members of their race. Notice that there is no calling of the police or National Guard. These white men apparently think that they can take this shit into their own hands. Besides that, the cops are all white anyway so why call your cousins or race-relatives since you know they're going to agree with whatever you do when the target or subject is a "black dick" that is out of control?

What about Shepperton, the man whose basement Prosser once lived in? The man who the neighbors considered to be Prosser's "owner"?

> Mr. Shepperton was already dressed. We saw him run down the
> back steps toward the carriage house. All three of us, Randy
> Nebraska, and myself, streaked down the alleyway to help him.
> We got the old wooden doors open. He went in and cranked the
> car. It was a new one, and started up at once. Mr. Shepperton
> backed out into the snowy drive. We all clambered up on the
> running board. He spoke absently, saying, "You boys stay here ...
> Randy, your mother's calling you," but we tumbled in and he
> didn't say a word.

They had a carriage house. Why was Prosser relegated to the basement? That carriage house could have been converted to a nice little apartment. Nope. White racism is the reason for the "shacks out back" during slavery. White racism is the reason for the "shanty towns" in some of these countries that they claim to feel so sorry for. White racism is the reason for the dilapidated buildings and houses and vacant lots in almost every ghetto in this country. They have a track record and they have a "type" of behavior when it comes to how to treat black people. Evidently, Thomas Wolfe is aware of it as he laid out the descriptions of Shepperton's house.

He tells the boys to stay behind, but they don't want to. He doesn't give a shit about their safety for the most part. He doesn't want them to witness the true nature of the white race and how it is going to come to the surface once they get their hands on (and bullets into) this nigga. The mob and the contagion continues to grow and spread, respectively:

> He came backing down the alleyway at top speed. We turned into the street and picked up Mr. Crane at the corner. We lit out for town, going at top speed. Cars were coming out of alleys everywhere. We could hear people shouting questions and replies at one another. I heard one man shout, "He's killed six men!" I don't think it took us over five minutes to reach the square, but when we got there, it seemed as if the whole town was there ahead of us. Mr. Shepperton pulled up and parked the car in front of the city hall. Mr. Crane leaped out and went pounding away across the square without another word to us.

This is true contagion, all this ire aimed at one brutha. They head to the town square and based on race, they have all congregated. This activity has a long history in small towns all across the south and the north. The hatred of black people is held within because of the service that is provided. As long as we can be able-bodied nannies, butlers, laborers, chauffeurs and so on, the white race is collectively satisfied. But a line from the movie "The Spook Who Sat By the Door" reveals a telling and important point: "The most invisible person in America is a nigga with a broom in his hand." And that remains true to this very day. Because of our lowly status, menial jobs and token titles, white people feel that can get "familiar" with us and therefore "know" us. Little do they know, as this short story proves and as the movie I just referred to depicts.

One black Dick who is predictably and understandably (at least to me) pissed off because of a history of being mistreated. And these white people act is if he is some monster attacking a small town ala the movie "Cloverfield." Check out the following:

> From every corner, every street that led into the square, people
> were streaking in. One could see the dark figures of running men
> across the white carpet of the square. They were all rushing in to
> one focal point. The southwest corner of the square where South
> Dean Street came into it was like a dog fight. Those running
> figures streaking toward that dense crowd gathered there made me
> think of nothing else so much as a fight between two boys upon the
> playgrounds of the school at recess time. The way the crowd was
> swarming in was just the same.

Yeah, but the comparison about the two school boys fighting doesn't include the variable of race. If it did, you'd see the same kind of school-oriented and community contagion taking place. And as can be expected, the black kid (who would probably be kicking the white kid's ass) would be grabbed, slapped around and ushered off to the principal's office. This case is a little different because the black person is an adult, out there on his own, far from the safe confines of "Niggertown," and these white people know it.

And the difference between a school boy fight and what is taking place in this case is seen even by the normally naïve white boys:

> But then I heard a difference. From that crowd came a low and
> growing mutter, an ugly and insistent growl,, of a tone and quality
> I had never heard before. But I knew instantly what it meant. There
> was no mistaking the blood note in that foggy growl. And we
> looked at one another with the same question in the eyes of all.
> Only Nebraska's coal-black eyes were shining now with a savage
> sparkle even they had never had before. "Come on," he said in a
> low tone, exultantly. "They mean business this time, sure. Let's
> go." And he darted away toward the dense and sinister darkness of
> the crowd.

The young white boy knows hate when he hears it. That is how to describe what he calls "Low and growing mutter," "blood note in that foggy growl," and so on. Again, we find the use of the terms "black" and "darkness" being associated with all that is negative. Wolfe, as a writer, is quite familiar with these terms and he has obviously bought into them. It's what I call "color-coded racism" and it permeates Anglo-American culture on all levels. Actually the term "sinister darkness" is redundant: in white culture, anything that has to do with "darkness" is automatically deemed or assumed to have a sinister quality.

Now we get to the "manhunt tradition" which I referred to earlier. Such madness continues, and as I wrote on November 24, 2005 in my article, "Pigmentation and the Pigskin,"

> Manhunt tradition – that's what Oliver C. Cox called it in his
> classic, Caste, Class and Race. Those folks were out to get Terrell
> to make an example of him. To them, he was an "uppity n------,"
> just like the NBA's Littrell Sprewell who wouldn't let a coach
> verbally abuse him, and just like wideout Keyshawn Johnson in
> 2003 – traded to another team when the coach couldn't "control"
> him. The media helps stigmatize Owens even more; almost every
> picture is one with a scowl, or Owens smelling his top lip. This is
> the same thing Time magazine did to O.J. Simpson and local
> newspapers do to black youth who are arrested. The worse they
> can make them look, the more physically menacing they can make
> them appear, the less empathy they'll get from society. (Stelly,
> 2007).

Is this not the strategy: the "paint" (or as they say "tar" or "taint") a potential victim with a brush that makes that human being into a monster of some kind so that collective white action can take place? This is what they did to the athletes mentioned in the previous excerpt and that is what Thomas Wolfe was doing in 1937 as he continued to create a "black monster" out of Prosser, a man who had formerly been humble to a fault. On to the manhunt:

> Even as we followed him, we hard coming toward us now,
> growing, swelling at every instant, one of the most savagely
> mournful and terrifying sounds that night can know. It was the
> baying of the hounds as they came up upon the leash from
> Niggertown. Full-throated, howling deep, the savagery of blood
> was in it, and the savagery of man's guilty doom was in it, too.

Getting bloodhounds after those who they are after – a typical mob tactic. And today's cops do the same thing with those German Shepherds that they have somehow managed to get the public to regard as "police officers." At any rate, history is best qualified to reward our research, as Malcolm X taught. My point here is that these white people, as it relates to their views on and reactions to issues of race, have changed very little since the times of antebellum slavery. The "baying of hounds" can be found in classic black works like Richard Wright's "Black Boy" and "Big Boy Goes Home."

But of course, in painting the fearsomeness of the hounds, Wolfe is also quick to add a little racism to the recipe where he writes, "Full-throated, howling deep, the savagery of blood was in it, and the savagery of man's guilty doom was in it, too." Now pay close attention because this peckerwood bastard is equating the alleged savagery of dogs with what he phrases as, "the savagery of man's guilty doom." No guilt has been established as far as they know. All they are going on are racist rumors. And how do they know he's doomed? What is this: an episode of "Have Gun Will Travel"? Prosser should be captured and brought before a court of law. But then again, he's black. And again, the Dred Scott decision rings most true: "A black man has no rights a white man is bound to respect." That was in 1857, and this story takes place in 1939 – eighty two years and the master-slave tradition is still in full effect.

The importance of property is made most clear in the following excerpt:

> They came up swiftly, airily baying at our heels as we sped across the snow-white darkness of the square. As we got up to the crowd, we saw that it had gathered at the corner where my uncle's hardware store stood. Cash Eager had not yet arrived, but, facing the crowd which pressed in on them so close and menacing that they were almost flattened out against the glass, three or four men were standing with arms stretched out in a kind of chain, as if trying to protect with the last resistance of their strength and eloquence the sanctity of private property.

Such collective cowardice! These white muthafuckas not only move as mobs after a single black man, but now they want to arm themselves. If the black man has a gun, then stay the fuck in the house. Who are these vigilante peckerwoods to chase down a brutha? This is a racist decision in and of itself. And since the cops are a part of it, this is a true manhunt, a true race-oriented search with the goal of taking the life of a black man. This is the classic definition of "bloodlust" – the uncontrollable desire to kill or maim others. They don't teach their young white kids about this side of the white man's "pioneer" spirit, do they? And now you know why: it doesn't just apply to hunting for food and resources – grizzlies, buffalo, wolves – it has also historically applied to black men and women, whether they committed a crime or not.

Continuing with the story:

> Will Henderson was mayor at that time, and he was standing there, arm to arm with Hugh McNair. I could see Hugh, taller by half a foot than anyone around him, his long gaunt figure, the aunt passion of his face, even the attitude of his outstretched bony arms, strangely, movingly Lincolnesque, his one good eye blazing in the cold glare of the corner lamp with a kind of cold inspired Scotch passion. "Wait a minute! You men wait a minute!" he cried. His words cut out above the clamor of the mob like an electric spark. "You'll gain nothing, you'll help nothing, if you do this thing!"

If there was ever any doubt about the intensity of racism and mob rule, when combined, merely document how these white people will treat their own fellow whites in order to "get that niggah!" History is replete with examples: from being called "nigger lover" to being shot or stabbed themselves, these white people are blinded when it comes to chasing down a black man. The ones who are acting as if they mob should "wait for the law to do its job" are only delaying the inevitable when it comes to race. The lynching will only be suspended temporarily. History is replete with examples of these law-abiding peckerwoods breaking into and tearing down jails to get at a black man who they believe needs to be lynched.

Moving on:

> They tried to drown him out with an angry and derisive roar. He shot his big fist up into the air and shouted at them, blazed at them with that cold single eye, until they had to hear. "Listen to me!" he cried. "This is no time for mob law! This is no case for lynch law! This is a time for law and order! Wait till the sheriff swears you in! Wait until Cash Eager comes! Wait --" He got no further. "Wait, hell!" cried someone. "We've waited long enough! We're going to get that nigger!"

The concept of "swearing in" peckerwoods like this is just one more example of white supremacy. How are you going to swear in ignorant hicks and empower them to hunt down another citizen? If that is the case, then of what good is law enforcement training? Of what use is the traditional police force? Don't get me wrong: all of this bullshit is racist to the core and in the case of the black man, the end result is going to be the same on some level – where white boys adopt the role of judge, jury and executioner. But I am addressing the amount of gall and temerity it takes to assume that an oath, a swearing in or even a badge and uniform, are going to make a peckerwood any less racist (or sexist) than he is as a regular citizen.

As Little Junior Brown (Nicholas Cage) said just before he blew the brains out of the unsuspecting undercover agent Omar (Ving Rhames) in the movie, "Kiss of Death," "Play with the bull, you get the horns." Following is another example of that principle at work:

> The mob took up the cry. The whole crowd was writhing angrily now, like a tormented snake. Suddenly there was a flurry in the crowd, scattering. Somebody yelled a warning at Hugh McNair. He ducked quickly, just in time. A brick whizzed past him, smashing the plate glass window into fragments. And instantly a blood roar went up. The crowd surged forward, kicked the fragments of jagged glass away. In a moment the whole mob was storming into the dark store.

The contagion was in full effect. The "bull" was seeing red (read: a nigga that needed to get got) and there would be no deterring them, even if it meant looting a store in front of young people. The owner of the store that these assholes had just broken into (and apparently looted) finally arrives:

> Cash Eager got there just too late. He arrived in time to take out his keys and open the front doors, but as he grimly remarked, it was like closing the barn doors after the horse had been stolen.

But that's okay. The horse that had been stolen was stolen by people who you know, who you trust, who you've lived next to for years. The "thieves" are people who, like you, share racist beliefs. And because the focus is "teaching that nigger a lesson," what you have in common with your fellow racists trumps any loss of property. That's how deep racism runs.

Moving right along,

> The mob was in and helped themselves to every rifle they could find. They smashed open cartridge boxes and filled their pockets with the loose cartridges. Within ten minutes, they had looted the store of every rifle, every cartridge, in the stock. The whole place looked as if a hurricane had hit it. The mob was streaming out into the street, was already gathering round the dogs a hundred feet or so away, who were picking up the scent at that point, the place where Dick had halted last before he had turned and headed south, downhill along South Dean Street toward the river.

A good sub-title for this would be, "In Search of a Black Dick." That's what all this is about, isn't it? Laws are allowed to be broken, rights can be violated, protocols trampled on, children traumatized – all because white men couldn't accept the fact that black people are human beings. And if you back any human being into a corner long enough, and make harassment and degradation a part of his daily schedule, then eventually that person is going to snap. It happened during antebellum slavery, so why wouldn't these small-town hicks believe that it couldn't happen to them? I'll tell you why: cultural arrogance, delusions of grandeur and white racism.

Using the dogs is a key part of the manhunt tradition. And there are studies about "white dogs," the ones who were trained to attack black people during the civil rights movement. But I did some research and I found that it wasn't just an American racist strategy. These kinds of dogs have been used in a number of racist contexts. Jeffery (2003) cogently contends that,

> Dogs can be trained to discriminate. Some Jamaican resorts feature dogs that chase blacks off the beach while leaving white frat boys to fry like bacon. South Africa's apartheid government bred "Boerbuls" by crossing Rottweilers, Dobermans, bloodhounds,

German shepherds, and even wolves to create very <u>aggressive</u> dogs for its security services. In the 1980s, the Herstigte Nasionale Party advertised such animals as "racist watchdogs" created "especially for South African circumstances."

This is not to say that the hounds in this story were of this ilk. It is merely to educate you, the reader, to the degree and depth that white people will go in order to control, oppress and regulate the behavior of people of color. And as you have read, it has been going on for some time. Furthermore,

In his 1982 film White Dog, director Sam Fuller explores the socialization of racism by having a black man attempt to retrain a dog taught to kill blacks—a so-called white dog—only to have the dog attack whites instead. Paramount found the film disturbing enough to block its release for more than a decade (Jeffery, 2003).

This point speaks volumes. Those with the power to block the release of films – Jewish controllers in Hollywood – will green light a movie because they know it will make money somewhere down the road. But when the issue strikes so close to home, it also contradicts that they say about being so "concerned" about black people and so "involved" in the civil rights movement. Although Jewish names may not appear in the credits, there is little doubt that Jews would have been in charge of production and distribution.

And here's a bit of trivia for ya: the man who wrote the story "White Dog" was a Russian-born writer named Romain Gary. What qualified him to write about racist dogs is beyond me, but I did learn that he fell for actress Jean Seberg (who was screwing brothers from the Black Panther Party) and when he found out that she was dating Clint Eastwood, he challenged Eastwood to a duel. Eastwood turned it down. Gary died of a self-inflicted gun wound. So even a nut can write a book that has some tidbits of truth.

Now, let us get away from the movie "White Dog" and get back to the two-legged "white dogs" that are hunting down a lone black man:

The hounds were scampering about, tugging at the leash, moaning softly with their noses pointed to the snow, their long ears flattened down. But in the light and in that snow it almost seemed no hounds were needed to follow Dick. Straight as a string, right down the center of the sheeted car tracks, the Negro's footsteps led away until they vanished downhill in the darkness. But now, although the snow had stopped, the wind was swirling through the street and making drifts and eddies in the snow. The footprints were fading rapidly. Soon they would be gone.

The writer underestimates the reason for the dogs. Sure, they were enlisted to track down Prosser. But they are also used to bite, butcher and maul him once he was found. At least, that's the way the mobs in the South used to use them when tracking down "an escaped nigrah." Showing that he is familiar with the terminology (and probably in agreement with the motivation of the mob), Wolfe offers the following:

> The dogs were given their head. They went straining on softly,
> sniffing at the snow; behind them the dark masses of the mob
> closed in and followed. We stood there watching while they went.
> We saw them go on down the street and vanish. But from below,
> over the snow-numbed stillness of the air, the vast low mutter of
> the mob came back to us.

Now consider for a moment, the impact that such observations are having on these small white boys. These kids were totally gullible and, despite the racism they had learned from their parents and neighbors. And now they were watching their elders break laws and violate protocols (e.g., innocent until proven guilty). They are seeing bloodlust in action and yet they will be taught Biblical bullshit in church and will be admonished in school if they dare to bully a classmate. Such hypocrisy cannot be forgotten by these young people. Today in 2016 many of them are at various stages of rebellion against what they see as the hypocrisy of their parents and the racism of their traditions. As they increasingly interact with black youth at school (certainly not in the segregated neighborhoods unless they drive down to go "slummin'") they learn more about just how fucked up their parents are and how devoid of truth their school curriculum is.

Moving on:

> Men were clustered now in groups. Cash Eager stood before is
> shattered window, ruefully surveying the ruin. Other men were
> gathered around the big telephone pole at the corner, pointing out
> two bullet holes that had been drilled cleanly through it. And
> swiftly, like a flash, running from group to group, like a powder
> train of fire, the full detail of that bloody chronicle of night was
> pieced together.

The white man's combination of fear and his love of his property perhaps know no equal. This muthafucka puts more priority on buildings, telephone poles and street signs than he does on his own family members. Look at the penalties that his laws reflect. Look at the creation of the neutron bomb: destroying human life while leaving buildings intact. And in order to paint a negative picture of the super villains and aliens in his movies, he shows his heroes tearing up entire cities which is aimed at pissing off the people who love the sky lines. Of particular interest should be the billions of dollars of property fucked up by the Avengers, Superman, and the Hulk.

With that bit of information out of the way, let us continue with the story, which now moves to explain why Prosser eventually "snapped" and started blowing people away:

> This is what had happened. Somewhere between nine and ten o'clock that night, Dick Prosser had gone to Pansy Harris's shack in Niggertown. Some say he had been drinking when he went there. At any rate, the police had later found the remnants of a gallon jug of raw corn whiskey in the room. What happened, what passed between them, was never known. And besides, no one was greatly interested. It was a crazy nigger with "another nigger's woman."

Let us analyze the preceding description and gain a deeper understanding of race relations, the racist mindset and the social interpretation of reality that is a product of both.

First of all, how did they know that Pansy Harris lived in a "shack"? Was this just an assumption because most of the people there lived in shacks? And why was this the case? Did they like their shacks or were they living in segregated conditions where the shacks, owned by white people, were all that they could afford?

Secondly, who are the people who say that he had been drinking, and since they didn't know for a fact, why even mention it? If they found "the remnants of a gallon jug of raw corn whiskey in the room," what does that mean? It doesn't prove that he was drinking that particular evening. But this is done to imply that the only way that a black man would have the guts to stand up to white people is if he was drunk or out of his head. This relieves white people by being able to believe this shit because a sober black man doing what Prosser did would send a *real* shiver up their pale spines.

Third and finally, the claim that no one really cared about what went on between Prosser and Pansy, adding that, "And besides, no one was greatly interested. It was a crazy nigger with "another nigger's woman." As long as it was black-on-black why should white people care; that is the purpose of segregation. To make sure that al that black anger and angst is handled inside the boundaries of "the ghetto" or "the slums" and doesn't spread outside to where "de good law abidin' white folks live."

One last point I want to make before we move on. This short story was undoubtedly assigned or read to young people while in school. Perhaps it was in a literature class or maybe in a class on writing. But make no mistake about it, white folks have heard this story before and they heard these words. And yet this short story and those like it are deemed "classics" by the people making curricular decisions for the schools. Some have come forward to attempt to edit the racist implications out of such stories and take out words like "nigger," "darkey," and others that denote race. But I oppose such a movement and here is why.

I want future generations to know what kind of low-life muthafuckas paved the way for their literature standards and protocols. I want them to know about the racism of Mark Twain, Thomas Wolfe, William Faulkner, Joseph Conrad and Ernest Hemingway – to name but a few. I want them to see the hypocrisy of that "One nation under God" bullshit that they swear to during athletic events, and what is taking place in the minds and imagery of their writers and historians. It is the only way for them to understand the inevitable collective ass kicking that this country is going to receive in the years ahead.

So Pansy and Prosser were fuckin' or something like that. And the story continues:

> Shortly after ten o'clock that night, the woman's husband appeared upon the scene. The fight did not start then. According to the woman, the real trouble did not come until an hour or more after his return. The men drank together. Each was in an ugly temper. Shortly before midnight they got into a fight. Harris slashed at Dick with a razor. In a second they were locked together, rolling about and fighting like two madmen on the floor. Pansy Harris went screaming out-of-doors and across the street into a dingy little grocery store.

This is a description of two men who knew one another and, more importantly, knew what Pansy was up to all along. That is why they took a break first, that is why they had a drink together, and that is why when they did re-unite, they got into a fight. More than likely it wasn't over Pansy because I doubt if either man really "wanted" her; it was more than likely over territoriality and the fact that Prosser was in this man's kitchen. He probably told Prosser to get the fuck out and Prosser probably said that he was invited, courtesy of Pansy. Who knows what took place? But here is what I do know.

I know that this peckerwood writer had no right referring to the fight that took place between these two men as "rolling about and fighting like two madmen." This perpetuates the myth of the "crazy nigger" and puts even more stereotype-based fear into the minds of the naïve reader, both black and white. The short story moves on:

> A riot call was telephoned at once to police headquarters on the public square. The news came in that a crazy nigger had broken loose in Gulley Street in Niggertown, and to send help at once. Pansy Harris ran back across the street toward her little shack. As she got there, her husband, with blood streaming from his face, staggered out into the street, with his hands held up protectively behind his head in a gesture of instinctive terror. At the same moment, Dick Prosser appeared in the doorway of the shack, deliberately took aim with his rifle and shot the fleeing Negro squarely through the back of the head. Harris dropped forward on his face into the snow. he was dead before he hit the ground. A huge dark stain of blood-soaked snow widened out around him.

So these bruthas are fighting and one thing leads to another one and Prosser shoots the brutha in the back of the head. Poor Harris never really had a chance. How did Prosser get his rifle into the situation? Was he in possession of it all along? If he was, what would prompt Harris to continue talking shit or to turn his back on Prosser? Had it stopped here and been black-on-black, those peckerwoods would not have cared. But as we will learn, Prosser wasn't in the mood or mental state to take any shit from *anyone*, black or white. Check it out:

> Dick Prosser seized the terrified negress by the arm, hurled her into the shack, bolted the door, pulled down the shades, blew out the lamp, and waited. A few minutes later, two policemen arrived from town. They were a young constable named Willis, and John Grady, a lieutenant of police. The policemen took one look at the bloody figure in the snow, questioned the frightened keeper of the grocery store, and after consulting briefly, produced their weapons and walked out into the street ...

The concept of "negress," as in female negro, is so colloquial and many dictionaries, as part of their definitions will include the fact that the term is "usually offensive." But this is Thomas Wolfe and the year is 1937 – this is the excuse that apologists will use.

At any rate two cops talk the store keeper, another black man, who is the one who phoned the cops and evidently Prosser knew about it. As we say today, "snitches get stitches." Willis must have been a rookie, a point that I believe is evidenced by the actions that follow:

> Young Willis stepped softly down onto the snow-covered porch of
> the shack. Flattened himself against the wall between the window
> and the door and waited. Grady went around to the side and
> flashed his light through the window, which, on this side, was
> shadeless. Grady said in a loud tone: "Come out of there!"

No identifying themselves as police officers, no notification that he is to come out with his hands up, and no mention of coming out unarmed. Just talking to Prosser like he's a dog, demanding him to "come out of there!" Without proper statements of who they are, why should he come out of his house? He doesn't recognize them as cops.

Here's the response they got:

> Dick's answer was to shoot him cleanly through the wrist. At the
> same moment Willis kicked the door in and without waiting,
> started in with pointed revolver. Dick shot him just above the eyes.
> The policeman fell forward on his face. Grady came running out
> around the house, pushed into the grocery store, pulled the receiver
> of the old-fashioned telephone off the hook, rang frantically for
> headquarters and yelled out across the wire that a crazy nigger had
> killed Sam Willis and a Negro man, and to send help.

Willis got a cap busted in his ass for trying to be the hog with the big nuts. He's going to kick in the door of a man that he believes to be armed and dangerous, a man who had not responded to his partners pronouncements? That is the sign of a rookie. And he got what a rookie gets when they make these kinds of mistakes. There is no way these white cops would have acted this way if the man that they suspected had been a white man.

With Willis flat on the floor dead as hell, Grady made a run for it and called for backup. Two men dead, one black and one white. The onslaught continues:

> At this moment Dick stepped out across the porch into the street,
> aimed swiftly through the dirty window of the little store, and shot
> John Grady as he stood there at the phone. Grady fell dead with a
> bullet that entered just below his left temple and went out the other
> side.

So now Grady got capped as he tried to call for backup. Prosser knew what he was doing and who he was doing it to. Dick is now on the move:

> Dick, now moving in a long, unhurried stride that covered the
> ground with catlike speed, turned up the long snow-covered slope
> of Gulley Street and began his march toward town. He moved right
> up the center of the street, shooting cleanly from left to right as he

> went. Halfway up the hill, the second-story window of a two-story
> Negro tenement flew open. An old Negro man stuck out his
> ancient head of cotton wool. Dick swiveled and shot casually from
> his hip. The shot tore the top of the old Negro's head off.

Again we find beastification terms as Dick is described as covering ground with "cat-like speed." Why couldn't he just be covering it quickly or rapidly? There is no way he was moving as fast as a cat, but to describe a black man's actions in relation to an animal of any kind is to "beastify" him and in doing so, make him less than human.

And what is this "ancient head of cotton wool" bullshit? White people have always been fascinated with the hair of black people and that which they cannot have or copy they defile or ridicule. They try to get perms but those are only temporary at best. Their women seek to make their lips fuller (like those of black women) by using various forms of lip augmentation (e.g., injections of restylane or artecoli) and who can forget the billion dollar sun tan industry? The "ancient head of cotton," as Wolfe described it, was shot off anyway.

Dick's odyssey of payback continues

> By the time Dick reached the head of Gulley Street, they knew he
> was coming. He moved steadily along, leaving his big tread
> cleanly in the middle of the sheeted street, shifting a little as he
> walked, swinging his gun crosswise before him. This was the
> Negro Broadway of the town, but where those poolrooms,
> barbershops, drugstores and fried-fish places had been loud with
> dusky life ten minutes before, they were now silent as the ruins of
> Egypt. The word was flaming through the town that a crazy nigger
> was on the way. No one showed his head.

Wolfe's racist references have no bounds. Let's analyze a few of them.

For one, the concept of a "Negro broadway" which is hardly a reference that black people created or would use. I sicken of these terms. When Muhammad Ali came out and announced the movie "The Greatest" back in __ the first thing that asshole said was that he was the "black Cary Grant." They used to refer to the beautiful Dorothy Dandridge as the "white Marilyn Monroe." The comparisons continue in an effort to sound flattering, but that's not what it is; it's white supremacy that makes white people and their "things" top of the totem pole and we come in as second-class peons, a "black version" of their alleged "greatness" and priorities.

Secondly, the businesses along the street being referred to as having been "loud with dusky life ten minutes before." Dusky is a term that you will find being used in reference to "negroes" in much of the early literature. What does it mean?

Being "dusky" is defined as, "dark in color; swarthy or dark-skinned." So being "loud with dusky life" means loud with black life? It means people talking, conversing and socializing, something that they are not allowed to do when white people are present? This is a racist statement and assumption that based on limited knowledge only.

Third, the fact that the businesses were no longer loud made them as "silent as the ruins of Egypt." The reason that Egypt was laid to ruin many centuries ago was because of white people who came in, saw the great structures, and lashed out at them like a gang of jealous bitches. They even shot the nose off of the Sphinx! One website source capsulizes the concept of these "ruins" by stating,

> Ancient Kemet (Ancient Egypt) was a 100% Black African built and ruled civilization. Despite all historical efforts by Eurocentric specialists to conceal, misrepresent, degrade, downplay and plagiarize this truth, Black African scholars and specialists have successfully refuted all systematic efforts to separate this great Black African history from Black African peoples worldwide. (Godlike Productions, 2010).

And as for the reference to "ruins," remember that ruins are buildings and structures that have been destroyed either by weather, time or by intentional attacks. In the case of Egypt, Europeans know what they did. To call any section of a place as being akin to "Egyptian ruins" without mentioning the role that white people played in the destruction of those landmarks is a gross distortion of reality (much like the contents of race relations in the story, "The Child By Tiger"!).

And fourth and finally, the word about a "crazy nigger was on the way" going through town. To be "crazy" or referred to as being crazy is to presume that the person mentally deranged on some level. The equation is simple: the man is a former vet, sent to fight a war that was about protecting the rights of the very same people who segregated and abused him upon his return. They live well and he lives an inferior life. He gets beaten just for being black and his entire race is relegated to a place called Niggertown. He has issues with a woman that was married and loses it, and then all these other negative memories come forward. That's not someone who is mentally deranged: that is someone who is sick and tired of white people and their wicked ways!

According to the story,

> Dick moved on steadily, always in the middle of the street, reached the end of Gulley Street, and turned into South Dean – turned right, uphill, in the middle of the car tracks, and started toward the square. As he passed the lunchroom on the left, he took a swift shot through the window toward the counter man. The fellow

ducked behind the counter. The bullet crashed into the wall above
his head.

Dick was out for blood, and he was ready to die. The counter man was probably someone who had insulted him in the past. He was out of the segregated black area and therefore everyone outside of it had to be white. And from his experience in the Army and based on what he had experienced at the hands of these "church-going white folk," he knew that they all shared the same anti-black mentality. Just as Nat Turner, during the slave rebellion told his followers to kill white babies too because "nits make lice," so to it was with what Prosser had decided to do. This was one "black Dick" that was not going to be forgotten!

And during all this, where were the cops?

> Meanwhile, at police headquarters, the sergeant had sent John Chapman out across the square to head Dick off. Mr. Chapman was perhaps the best-liked man on the force. He was a pleasant florid-faced man of forty-five, with curling brown mustaches, congenial and good-humored, devoted to his family, courageous, but perhaps too kindly and too gentle for a good policeman. John Chapman heard the shots and ran. He came up to the corner by Eager's hardware store just as Dick's last shot went crashing through the lunchroom window.

We know that Chapman was a white man because a "florid-faced man" is a man whose face is flushed. He's white and that's why he's described as being "pleasant," "congenial," "good humored," "courageous" and even "Perhaps too kindly and gentle" to be a good cop. That is how white folks see him because that is the way he acts toward them. Ask black people if this muthafucka acts that way if he happens to venture into Niggertown. As black men if he's so "congenial" when he enters a black bar or night club. Ask black people what Chapman's views were on treating black people with some dignity. You don't judge a peckerwood based on how he treats his fellow crackers; you look at how he acts towards "the least of these" and then you make your decision about his character and personality.

At any rate, Chapman hears the shots and what does he do? He sets up an ambush! Where is all that courage that was bestowed upon him in the previous paragraph? Where is the bravado? Where is all that kindness? Check out Chapman's response to Prosser in this situation:

> Mr. Chapman took up his post there at the corner behind the telephone post that stood there at that time. Mr. Chapman, **from his vantage point behind the post,** took out his revolver **and shot**

> **directly at Dick Prosser as he came up the street.** By this time
> Dick was **not more than thirty yards away**. He dropped quietly
> on one knee and aimed. **Mr. Chapman shot again and missed**.
> Dick fired. The high-velocity bullet bored through the post a little
> to one side. It grazed the shoulder of John Chapman's uniform and
> knocked a chip out of the monument sixty years or more behind
> him in the center of the square. (emphasis added)

Chapman was trying to kill this brutha! He was not bullshittin'! There was none of that "shoot to wound" thinking on is mind! He protected himself like the gutless snipers that this country glorifies during times of war, and took a shot to kill Prosser. But he fucked up even though he had him literally at point blank range. Then he shot again. So this nice guy that everybody likes and who has all these good qualities was just like far too many of the police officers to this very day: not qualified to do the job once they hit the streets. And once the variable of race is interjected into these equations, most of these peckerwoods get a case of the nerves and flip into that "kill the nigger at all costs" mode and what happens is that they start shaking and missing the target.

Chapman was on a kill mission, but he fucked up. Here's what happened next:

> Mr. Chapman fired again and missed. And Dick, still coolly poised
> upon is knee, as calm and as steady as if he were engaging in rifle
> practice, fired again, drilled squarely through the center of the post
> and shot John Chapman through the heart. Then Dick rose, pivoted
> like a soldier in his tracks, and started down the street, straight as a
> string, right out of town. This was the story as we got it, pieced
> together like at rain of fire among the excited groups of men that
> clustered there in trampled snow before the shattered glass of
> Eager's store.

So to use the analogy of the penis for a moment, what we have is a Black Dick ejaculating into the forehead of the white man and killing him. The dick then gets erect and prepares for his next conquest! The previous passage pays tribute to the army as being at the basis of Prosser's actions, but the army should be credited with something that is not so much behavioral as psychological: that being how to focus on killing an enemy who is out to kill you, especially if the enemy is one that has done you harm in the past. And this is what Prosser was doing.

Back at the store:

> But now, save for these groups of talking men, the town again was
> silent. Far off in the direction of the river, we could hear the
> mournful baying of the hounds. There was nothing more to see or

do. Cash Eager stooped, picked up some fragments of the shattered glass, and threw them in the window. A policeman was left on guard, and presently all five of us – Mr. Shepperton, Cash Eager, and we three boys – walked back across the square and got into the car and drove home again.

There is nothing more pitiful than white people who are looking for a reason as to why they are so pitiful. The reasons are staring them right in the face! They think their problems stem from the lack of hair, or the need for a tan, or perhaps even a better paying job. This may be part of it, but it is not the core reason as to why, as a collective, they are such a pitiful, albeit powerful, lot. The reason is that they are cowardly, and always have been. Even with the great armies of the past, they were cowards when it came to the simple things: accepting people and cultures who are different, treating their women like human beings, and so on. And because of these issues (and several more) they tremble in the face of obstacles and are left, in many cases, being too weak to do anything but wander – like the five people we just read about.

But there was no more sleep, I think for anyone that night. Black Dick had murdered sleep. Toward daybreak, snow began to fall again. The snow continued through the morning. It was piled deep in gusting drifts by noon. All footprints were obliterated; the town waited, eager, tense, wondering if the man would get away. They did not capture him that day, but they were on his trail …

No, Black Dick is not the one who murdered the sleep of these white people. They did it to themselves. It's strange that they slept perfectly well knowing that there was a section of their town that they casually referred to as "Niggertown." They slept just fine knowing that within that segregated enclave there were people suffering from a plethora of social ills that were largely placed there by poverty that, in turn, was imposed by their fellow whites. These white folks slept just fine knowing that what they have is the residue of what which was stolen, sold and auctioned off from Native Americans. But when a lone black man seeks payback, all of a sudden these white muthafuckas are experiencing sleeplessness. Go drink a bottle of Nyquil and shut the fuck up!

Prosser had made it past the first day and was still on his feet. And the wary and wily white boys were still had it, accompanies by hounds and handguns, working diligently to weed out this "nigger" who had to be taught "his place." Rumors, combined with what they called "news," continued to inundate the small town:

> From time to time throughout the day, news would drift back to us.
> Dick had turned east along the river and gone out for some miles
> along the Fairchilds road. There, a mile or two from Fairchilds, he
> crossed the river at the Rocky Shallows.

Please note that these cowardly white people are getting news, probably by phone or maybe local radio, that Prosser is on the prowl. But how many of them have the balls to get up and do something about this perceived threat? How many of these brave white men who go to the movies and see the stars of the late 1930s like Melvyn Douglas, Spencer Tracy, John Wayne, Edward G. Robinson, James Cagney and William Holden. And how about the macho men of the 1940s: the likes of Humphrey Bogart, Gregory Peck, Cornel Wilde and the like? The images on the screen are a long way from the white man in reality, are they not? And what Wolfe is writing about is a reflection of what he (Wolfe) knows about his race; akin to Superman adopting the identity of a "mild mannered reporter" because that is how he perceived men from earth: mild mannered, clumsy and naïve.

Moving on with the story:

> Shortly after daybreak, a farmer from the Fairchilds section had
> seen him cross a field. They picked the trail up there again and
> followed it across the field and through a wood. He had come out
> on the other side and got down into the Cane Creek section, and
> there, for several hours, they lost him. Dick had gone right down
> into the icy water of the creek and walked upstream a mile or so.
> They brought the dogs down to the creek, to where he broke the
> trail, took them over to the other side, and scented up and down.

The hatred that this black man feels for his oppressors appears to know no bounds. He's trudging through ice cold water, and for what reason? He can't be hoping to get away, so he's just looking for a better position where he can expend all of his bullets busting caps in the asses of any white boys stupid enough to venture his way. The hunt was on – and Dick Prosser was the prey. But when you look at it, he didn't feel that way – the white folks did. They were hunting in fear, the way you see those white boys do in the old movies when they hunt for the Frankenstein monster or for the tomb of Count Dracula.

Moving on:

> Toward five o'clock that afternoon they picked the trail up on the
> other side, a mile or more upstream. From that point on, they
> began to close in on him. The dogs followed him across the fields,
> across the Lester road, into a wood. One arm of the posse swept
> around the wood to head him off. They knew they had him. Dick,
> freezing, hungry, and unsheltered, was hiding in that wood. They

knew he couldn't get away. The posse ringed the wood and waited
until morning.

Like vultures over the dying prey, these peckerwoods are not thinking about
"capturing" Prosser. They are not even considering bringing him in alive for trial.
Nope. Not when the person in question is black. He can forget anything even
remotely resembling justice. And is this not the way it is today on a more
technological, expeditious and straight-forward level when these cops
"accidentally on purpose" gun down black youth in the streets, harass black
women and then lynch them while they're in jail, haphazardly pump 16 rounds into
the body of a black teenager, or just simply bust a cap in the back of a black man
who is running away. The story took place in the late 1930s, and what I have just
described are actual incidents from 2015 – some 75 years later. In simpler terms,
"the posse" mentality and the manhunt tradition are still alive and well. And the
primary targets remain black and brown people.

The night passed and the cat-and-mouse "game" continued:

> At 7:30 the next morning he made a break for it. He got through
> the line without being seen, crossed the Lester road, and headed
> back across the field in the direction of Cane Creek. And there they
> caught him. They saw him plunging through the snowdrift of a
> field. A cry went up. The posse started after him. Part of the posse
> were on horseback. The men rode in across the field. Dick halted at
> the edge of the wood, dropped deliberately upon one knee, and for
> some minutes held them off with rapid fire. At two hundred years
> he dropped Doc Lavender, a deputy, with a bullet through the
> throat.

What a courageous black man. But I'm willing to bet you apples to oranges
that not a single peckerwood reading or listening to this story, at least not under the
age of ten, would see it that way. And that is the purpose: Wolfe wanted to paint
Dick Prosser as a beast, replete with the frequent references to Black Dick and to
animals. And this is how it came to pass. The posse closes in on a lone black man
and to far too many white folks, this is fair and the way it should be.

Moving right along:

> The posse came in slowly, in an encircling, flankwise movement.
> Dick got two more of them as they closed in, and then, as
> deliberately as a trained soldier retreating in good order, still firing
> as he went, he fell back through the wood. At the other side he
> turned and ran down through a sloping field that bordered on Cane
> Creek. At the creek edge, he turned again, knelt once more in the
> snow, and aimed.

It is clear that Prosser was going to "go out swinging." He knew white people and he surely knew that by now, he had pissed them off. After all, they showed him disrespect and disdain all those years when he was kissing their ass, so he couldn't fare much worse. Continuing:

> It was Dick's last shot. He didn't miss. The bullet struck Wayne Foraker, a deputy, dead center in the forehead and killed him in his saddle. Then the posse saw the Negro aim again, and nothing happened. Dick snapped the breech open savagely, then hurled the gun away. A cheer went up. The posse came charging forward. Dick turned, stumblingly, and ran the few remaining yards that separated him from the cold and rock-bright waters of the creek.

Cowardly bastards. The white man being held off by one black man. And that is a metaphor for the way it has been in a number of instances that have gone unreported. And why? Because they are ashamed. They do not want their cowardice to become a matter of public record. That is why they spend billions promoting their military might, how "great" their respective police forces are and even sprinkle in a little mythology where white people actually have super powers, the ability to fly and so on. Only when the black man's gun is out of ammunition do these white men, on horseback and assisted with bloodhounds, come "charging forth."

From there, the story informs us more about the situation:

> And here he did a curious thing – a thing that no one ever wholly understood. It was thought that he would make one final break for freedom, that he would wade the creek and try to get away before they got to him. Instead, he sat down calmly on the bank, and as quietly as if he were seated on his cot in an Army barracks, he unlaced his shoes, took them off, placed them together neatly at his side, and then stood up like a soldier, erect, in his bare bleeding feet, and faced the mob.

Prosser went down with dignity. It was clear that he had humiliated the mob, eluded them, took a number of them out in the process. The white man could not understand it, not that he would not do it if in the presence of an enemy. But that he didn't think that a black man had the courage or mentality to do it. This has been the white man's main weakness when it came down to interactions with black men: he continues to underestimate people because of the racial makeup of nonwhite people.

The manhunt tradition continues:

> The men on horseback reached him first. They rode up around him
> and discharged their guns into him. He fell forward in the snow,
> riddled with bullets. The men dismounted, turned him over on his
> back, and all the other men came in and riddled him.. They took
> his lifeless body, put a rope around his neck, and hung him to a
> tree. Then the mob exhausted all their ammunition on the riddled
> carcass.

Riddled with bullets. This was so typical of white boys no matter what the geographic milieu. Check out a book by Ralph Ginzburg called *100 Years of Lynchings*. It's a collection of newspapers clippings, replete with headlines, that document the things that these white men did to black men. And one of the most common "side dishes" that was served along with the main course of the lynch rope around the neck was that of riddling the body with bullets.

In this case they concluded with the actual lynching and then shot the body up again. How sick can you get, even when it comes to someone you hate? How can these white people who claim to be Christians, debase another one of their God's creatures in such a way? How can white bitches marry and remain hooked up with men who are so savage and cowardly? Another thing you will learn when you study the history of such mob actions was that in many cases they would cut the body down and then sell body parts in the local store, ranging from fingers and toes to an occasion dick or nut sack (scrotum).

Dick Prosser had been eviscerated, mutilated and exterminated. According to the story, the mob was not yet done:

> By nine o'clock that morning the news had reached the town.
> Around eleven o'clock, the mob came back along with river road.
> A good crowd had gone out to meet it at the Wilton Bottoms. The
> sheriff rode ahead. Dick's body had been thrown like a sack and
> tied across the saddle of the horse of one of the deputies he had
> killed.

Who was the sick fuck that was assigned to pick up the black man's bloody body and place it across the saddle of a horse? How could anyone who read this story and realized that it was not an original piece but something borrowed from actual history, still as yet believe that the white race was nothing more than a group of savages? Have you read any historical information of black people, Latinos, Asians or anyone doing such a thing to an innocent white man or woman? Even the Native Americans, who had every reason to butcher white people, would only do so in response to some barbaric attack by white males where they would murder Native children and women.

And such activity was par for the course. As evidence let me share with you the case of Claude Neal. According to historical sources and my own research,

> Claude Neal was an African American farmhand living in Jackson County, Florida who was accused of raping and murdering Lola Cannady, a nineteen-year-old white female, just outside the town of Greenwood on October 18, 1934. Neal was arrested and charged for the crime and despite a lack of sufficient evidence against him to prove his guilt beyond a reasonable doubt, lynch mobs began to form to find and kill him. In order to keep Neal safe from the lynch mobs he was moved to multiple jails but was finally captured and brought back to Marianna, Florida. Neal was then tortured and finally killed by a group of lynchers and the body was brought to the Cannady farm where it was further mutilated by those who had come to witness the lynching.

And the similarities don't end there, folks:

> The body was later hung in front of the Marianna courthouse before being cut down and buried by the sheriff in the morning.[3] A large group of people came to the courthouse and made demands to see the body be hung up again and eventually started attacking blacks in the area and rioting. The lynching of Claude Neal and the riots that followed played a large part in bringing about the end of the practice of lynching in the United States (Younglbood, 2007).

Wolfe's "idea" and the short story that followed was therefore hardly unique. His descriptions would and could have been found in any newspaper account of the lynching of a black person. I provided the case of Claude Neal to prove to you that this is the reality.

Next comes what I refer to as "the degradation campaign." And these are the actions which clearly show the raw savagery of this white community and, in my view, white communities all over this nation during this time period:

> It was this way, bullet-riddled, shot to pieces, open to the vengeful and morbid gaze of all, that Dick came back to town. The mob came back right to its starting point in South Dean Street. They halted there before au undertaking parlor, not twenty yards away from where Dick had killed John Chapman. They took that ghastly mutilated thing and hung it in the window of the undertaker's place, for every woman, man and child in town to see.

Even in death it is Prosser's body – the body of the "black Dick" – that is blamed and viewed as problematic. For instance, the writer, Wolfe, refers to the body as being open "to the vengeful and morbid gaze of all." This man is a wordsmith, and he is aware of what was really taking place, even in his warped mind. He knows that he is leaving out a key word: "hateful." Those white people had already gotten their revenge with icing on top! But what they were feeling and exhibiting, just by the fact that the body was being displayed for all to see, was raw, unadulterated "race hatred."

So hateful where they that they "honored" their kill by bringing the body of the "prey" back to the original spot where the killing started. Even in death, the last insult by the writer was hurled at the black man by referring to his dead body as "that ghastly mutilated thing." But if that was the case, why was it then hung in a window, and get this, hung there "for every women, man and child in town to see." What race of people acts in such a manner? What community, even with its own police force, would behave and get approval for what just took place? So when white people are on television lecturing about equality, truth, justice and the American way, it is incumbent upon you to remind them that this short story is not some "Star Wars" figment of the white imagination: *it is rooted in and borrowed from actual historical fact.* And that is the greatest horror story of all.

The macabre aftermath of the hateful hacking apart of the black man by the horse riding honkies can now take place.

> And it was so we saw him last. We said we wouldn't look. But in the end we went. And I think it has always been the same with people. They protest. They shudder. And they say they will not go. But in the end they always have their look. At length we went. We saw it, tried wretchedly to make ourselves believe that once this thing had spoken to us gently, had been partner to our confidence, object of our affection and respect. And we were sick with nausea and fear, for something had come into our lives we could not understand.

How duplicitous are these peckerwoods? The man from whom they learned so much was now just a "thing." And then they back it up with the false claim that, "we were sick with nausea and fear, for something had come into our lives we could not understand." Bullshit! You understand why Prosser did what he did! But the truth is you did not want to *accept* what you understood. The man who beats his wife and then comes back and apologizes telling her, "look what you made me do." The parents who abuses a child and tells the child that it's for "their own good." This is the kind of warped thinking that serves as model behavior for kids like the ones in this story. *They have been taught by centuries of white experts, how to lie about reality and no matter what happens, all white action against nonwhites is, on some level, justified.*

Like the assholes who slow down on the interstate to look over at a car accident hoping to spot a mangled body, so it has always been in this country. And the mutilation of a black man by a white mob was no exception. Check it out:

> We looked and whitened to the lips, and craned our necks and looked away, and brought unwilling, fascinated eyes back to the horror once again, and craned and turned again, and shuffled in the slush uneasily, but could not go. And we looked up at the leaden reek of day, the dreary vapor of the sky, and, bleakly, at these forms and faces all around us – the people come to gape and stare, the poolroom loafers, the town toughs, the mongrel conquerors of the earth – and yet, familiar to our lives and to the body of our whole experience, all known to our landscape, all living men.

The people came to gape and stare. No black person in his right mind would dare to venture forth because they knew their "place" and this incident surely drove home that point. To these white people it was "all niggers" this and "all niggers" that. And now there would be fear throughout the black community for months until things became calm again. But the rumors of what "that nigger Dick Prosser" did will live, become exaggerated, and then reach the status of legend.

And with that legend will come the white version of reality, one that will continue to be skewed with bullshit, tombstone courage, false bravado and their usual racist analyses. Take note of the following:

> And something had come into life – into our lives – that we had never known about before. It was a kind of shadow, a poisonous blackness filled with bewildered loathing. The now would go, we knew, the reeking vapors of the sky would clear away. The leaf, the blade, the bud, the bird, then April would come back again, and all of this would be as it had ever been. The homely light of day would shine gain familiarly. And all of this would vanish as an evil dream. And yet not wholly so. For we would still remember the old dark doubt and loathing of our kind, of something hateful and unspeakable in the souls of men. We knew that we should not forget.

The preceding is an attempt to make it appear as if the white man has a conscience when it comes to savagery such as that which was shown against Dick Prosser. But facts are facts; just because you have a memory of a barbaric act doesn't mean you have any truly deep feelings about it. Even in describing it you can see the same color-coded racism that writers like Wolfe have been and continue to be: "And yet not wholly so. For we would still remember the old dark doubt and loathing of our kind, of something hateful and unspeakable in the souls of men. We knew that we should not forget." "Old DARK doubt." Doubts that are negative, of course. But as for the "loathing of their kind," that is bullshit. You might despise the action (which I doubt), but white supremacy and race hate haven't existed for as long as they have with the white man hating his own people for displaying and acting out on these things.

Now all of a sudden these muthafuckas become creatures of compassion and deep thought. Check it out:

> Beside us a man was telling the story of his won heroic accomplishments to a little group of fascinated listeners. I turned and looked at him. It was Ben Pounders of the ferret face, the furtive and uneasy eye, Ben Pounders of the mongrel mouth, the wry muscles of the jaw, Ben Pounders the collector of usurious lendings to the blacks, the nigger hunter. And now Ben Pounders boasted of another triumph. He was the proud possessor of another scalp.

It sounds to me as if Ben Pounders was a Jew. He was loaning out money at huge interest rates to black people, which means he was making a profit. If not for that he couldn't care less about black people when they were alive and well. So why in the fuck would he be boasting about the death of a black man and how he had a souvenir of a black man who had been riddled with bullets? I'll tell you why: because he's a sick fuck. The white man has always bitten the hand that feeds him. He does it with his own woman (hence, spousal abuse, rapes and assaults), he does it with his children (pedophilia, child abuse), and he does it to employees who work for him but he summarily fires if it threatens his real love, which is the bottom line.

Take note that the narrator/writer, the young boy, has a lot to say in his description of Pounder, including referring to the grown man as "the nigger hunter." But he was along on the trip, as were his pals. They had to witness the mutilated body as it hung in the window of the store. In criminal law there is a thing called "aiding and abetting." These young butt wipes were as guilty and as complicit in the "lynching" of Dick Prosser as the adult whites. And this is something that white people claim to not be able to understand: they may not have directly kidnapped and enslaved black people during the development of the slave system, but indirectly this nation, every peckerwood in it, has benefited from it. And they don't and cannot deny that it existed. But they don't want to accept responsibility for it. The same can be said for the thievery of land from the Native Americans.

In simpler terms, I don't see men like Pounder as some kind of "racist exception." I see him as typical and as being a part of it. He's just like the cop that doesn't shoot down black kids in the streets, but hears the bragging coming from the ones who do it. And yet he does nothing. This "code of silence" therefore makes him complicit in the act and the cover-up.

Back to Pounder and his pontificating:

> "I was the first one to git in a shot," he said. "You see that hole there?" He pointed with a dirty finger. "That big hole right above the eye?" They turned and goggled with a drugged and feeding stare. "That's mine," the hero said, turned briefly to the side and spat tobacco juice into the slush. "That's where I got him. Hell, after that he didn't know what hit him. He was dead before he hit the ground. We all shot him full of holes then. We sure did fill him full of lead. Why, hell yes," he declared, with a decisive movement of his head, "we counted up to two hundred and eighty-seven. We must have put three hundred holes in him."

Now to put this into perspective, when the FBI bushwhacked Bonnie and Clyde back in 1934 near Sailes, Louisiana, there were 150 shots put into the car that they were in and when they pulled the bodies out, it was a mesh of blood and flesh. So in other words, the body of Dick Prosser was hit with almost double that amount. And why do you think that was? First of all, Clyde Barrow and Bonnie were white legends that were worshipped despite their crimes. Secondly, Clyde had a woman with him, even if she was the brains of the outfit. And third, they were white, and no matter how much money they stole or how many people they killed, they were nowhere near guilty of the ultimate crime: the "crime" of being "a nigger." As Sly and the Family Stone sang in their cut "Everyday People," "Different strokes for different folks."

In an attempt to show that there was a white man who had some semblance of conscience, the story describes the following:

> And Nebraska, fearless, blunt, outspoken, as he always was, turned abruptly, put two fingers to his lips, and spat between them, widely and contemptuously. "Yeah – *we!*" he grunted. "*We* killed a big one! We – we killed a ba'r, we did! ... Come now, boys," he said gruffly. "Let's be on our way!" And fearless and unshaken, untouched by any terror or any doubt, he moved away. And two white-faced nauseated boys went with him.

Now they want to equate a black man with being a "bear." Again, we have beastification akin to that which I pointed our earlier. And as I said, this mentality continues to pervade American society. The only difference being that today we aid and abet society in that kind of belief system: athletes referring to themselves as being "in beast mode" or constituting "a stable of running backs." Coaches making statements about "reining in" the athletes or young athletes being "colts" or a team being "horses." It goes on and on and I've pointed it out in major manuscripts I've written over the years. The point has been well-made: black people prior to, during and since enslavement have always been deemed "less than human" – oftentimes beastlike – by white people.

What could be referred to as "the legend of the dead nigger" continues as Wolfe writes that,

> A day or two went by before anyone could go into Dick's room again. I went in with Randy and his father. The little room was spotless, bare, and tidy as it had always been. But even the very austerity of that little room now seemed terribly alive with the presence of its black tenant. It was Dick's room. We all knew that. And somehow we all knew that no one else could ever live there again.

How could these peckerwoods "know" that no one would ever live there again? The white man will do anything for income, and renting out that room is no exception. These muthafuckas rent out houses that have had mass murders and butchering that take place in them; drug deals and police shootouts. All they do is hire a contractor to patch up the bullet holes, repair a few doors and windows, slap on a new paint job and voila! Rental property! It wasn't even "Dick's room" when he was living there; it was the white man's room, he was just frontin' Dick's black ass off!

To have this paragraph included is once again an attempt to make it appear as if the white kids feel regret, remorse or have a conscience. That is not the case: it is fear. Even the white man and boy, with their heinous history, know well and understand the law of karma: what goes around comes around. And that is the basis of their fear of black people even today. They know what they have done in the past and that the past is prologue. That is why they spend so much money on preventive measures to ensure that black people never get in the position to do to them what they've done to us. Fear is not the same as remorse or regret.

As evidence, take note the Biblical reference:

> Mr. Shepperton went over to the table, picked up Dick's old Bible that still lay there, open and face downward, held it up to the light, and looked at it, at the place that Dick had marked when he last read in it. And in a moment, without speaking to us, he began to read in a quiet voice:
> "The Lord is my shepherd; I shall not want.
> "He maketh me to lie down in green pastures: he leadeth me beside the still waters.

> "He restoreth my soul: he leadeth me in the paths of righteousness
> for his name's stake.
> "Yea, though I walk through the valley of the shadow of death, I
> will fear no evil: for thou art with me -- "

And Dick understood what he had to do. I don't buy into all this "Lord is my shepherd" bullshit because I am nobody's sheep, cow or lamb. But I understand the metaphorical significance of "walking through the valley of the shadow of death" because Black people, we do it with every waking minute. And Dick Prosser did it as well, and he knew he was doing it. His rampage had nothing to do with Pansy or pussy: it had to do with having had enough of these white people, observing how they live and how hypocritical they were to ritually attend church, talk about God and Jesus, and then maintain a "special section" of town reserved for black people, a section of town that was intentionally under-developed and stigmatized.

After reading that verse, life goes on as Wolfe writes that, "Then Mr. Shepperton closed the book and put it down upon the table, the place where Dick had left it. And we went out the door, he locked it, and we went back into that room no more forever." The word "forever" is one more example of white grandiosity: as if they can control time and space. He doesn't speak for members of the Shepperton family; there is not a room in that house that will remain closed down or locked "forever." White people don't waste space, and the death of a "nigger" is not enough for them to see that space translates into possible revenue and if not that, then some place that can become a guest room for a relative or family friend. Who does Thomas Wolfe think he's fooling with his bullshit embellishments?

Continuing:

> The years passed, and all of us were given unto time. We went our
> ways. But often they would turn and come again, these faces and
> these voices of the past, and burn there in my memory again, upon
> the muted and immortal geography of time.

You can only recall reality based upon the impact that it has had on you. If these voices of the past were burned into his memory, then the main voice should have been of his fellow whites and their maniacal screams of "get that nigger!" He was a part of it. He helped celebrate it by viewing the body. He helped confirm it by never speaking out against how wrong it was. He kept the secret about Dick having the gun and about the promise. He and his friends fucked up on their racist obligation to tell their white elders that "the nigger" had not only showed them how to shoot a gun but promised to do so again in the future.

What he is describing is not the same thing as guilt. In my view a guilty conscience can be addressed or assuaged by going out and doing something about it. Just because you re-hash what you saw, heard and were involved in doesn't mean that you regret having been involved. It just seems that in some small way you've come to the realization that, as a collective, your elders and good friends are nothing more than white racists without bed sheets on. And *that* is the reality that you have got to deal with and accept.

Moving on:

> And all would come again – the shout of the young voices, the
> hard thud of the kicked ball, and Dick moving, moving steadily,
> Dick moving, moving silently, a storm-white world and silence,
> and something moving, moving in the night. Then I would hear the
> furious bell, the crowd a-clamor and the baying of the dogs, and
> feel the shadow coming that would never disappear. Then I would
> see again the little room that we would see no more, the table and
> the book. And the pastoral holiness of that old psalm came back to
> me, and my heart would wonder with perplexity and doubt.

And just think: there is a race of people out there who participated in, witnessed and glorified lynchings of black people. They are now older and perhaps may or may not have shared it with their grandchildren or great-grandchildren. But there are hundreds of thousands of them who know how low white people can stoop; not only in times of war, but against innocent people simply because of the color of their skin.

But not even the Psalm can over-rule racism. Wolfe writes above that, "And the pastoral holiness of that old psalm came back to me, and my heart would wonder with perplexity and doubt." Not regret. Not remorse. Not hatred of the act that took place. But perplexity, which means he was puzzled and doubt, which means he wasn't sure if he knew what to think. These are cover-ups and veils that white people wear because their history is so repulsive that they have to revise it, lie about it or pretend that only the positive things took place. That is what their education system, their media and their museums are all about: *show how good and great we were and during times of violence, provide us with a good reason for using it.*

Following is what I view as a key component of the short story:

> For I had heard another song since then, and one that Dick, I know,
> had never heard, and one perhaps he might not have understood,
> but one whose phrases and imagery it seemed to me would suit
> him better:

What the hammer? What the chain?
In what furnace was thy brain?
What the anvil? What dread grasp
Dare its deadly terrors clasp?

When the stars threw down their spears
And water'd heaven with their tears
Did He smile His work to see?
Did he who made the lamb make thee?

This poem is called, "The Tyger," and was written by another racist named William Blake. Blake was a racist muthafucker. In a poem he called, "Black Boy," we find a poem beginning with a black boy comparing himself to a white boy and basically saying that he is "bereav'd of light" because he is black, but that the white boy is angelic." Say what? There are apologists who claim that Blake was anti-slavery and anti-racism. I say that a man is the sum of his functions: if that muthafucka wrote and believed what I just shared, then there is nothing "anti-racist" about him.

In his analysis of "The Tyger," it seems that Wolfe and I are again in disagreement where he claims, "*What* the hammer? *What* the chain?" No one ever knew. It was a mystery and a wonder." The fact is that Dick Prosser "put the hammer down" on those peckerwoods before they killed him, didn't he?! And he fucked with their minds and lives to the point where rumors persisted long after his death. For instance,

> There were a dozen stories, a hundred clues and rumors; all came to nothing in the end. Some said that Dick had come from Texas, others that his home had been in Georgia. Some said it was true that he had been enlisted in the Army, but that he had killed a man while there and served a term at Leavenworth. Some said he had served in the Army and had received an honorable discharge, but had later killed a man and had served a term in a state prison in Louisiana. Others said that he had been an Army man, but that he had gone crazy, that he had served a period in an asylum when it was found that he was insane, that he had escaped from this asylum, that he had escaped from prison, that he was a fugitive from justice at the time he came to us.

I have thought and believed, for a long time, that the white male is very much like a bitch. The qualities he abhors about his woman are qualities that he possesses. He says a woman's role is to cook, yet the best chefs in the world are men. He says a woman is supposed to sew and darn socks, and yet he is the fashion designer who steals ideas and then sends them down the runway telling women what is in vogue. And she's supposed to be the giddy, gossipy one who runs her mouth non-stop, and yet who do you think was spreading the rumors about Dick Prosser that you just read above? White men, that's who.

Bitches with dicks. The white man's frequent conniptions (e.g., Donald Trump, Vladimir Putin), bitch-like admiration of the physicality of other men (mainly blacks) as heard in the emotion-laden announcing of Brent Musberger, Marv Albert, Joe Buck, Al Michaels, Dick Vitale, Chris Collinsworth, Jim McKay, Terry Bradshaw, Bill Walton, Phil Simms, Dan Patrick – to name but a few) and general demeanor paint a picture of someone who talks about masculinity but far too often displays quasi-feminine characteristics when he becomes emotional.

Now let's look at a few of the rumors posted above and attempt to provide some semblance of logic to them, logic from a black perspective (mine) not from some racist white revisionist interpreter.

By believing that Prosser came from the South, the stereotypical white folks believed that he had already been "broken in." That is what the South has produced: groups of docile and accommodationist black folks. Even to this day when these white school districts like the Omaha Public Schools go out recruiting for teachers, they head to the South. Why? Because that is where they are going to find the kind of black people who will accept low salaries (at least the salaries are higher than what the South offers), and will follow orders and be submissive in the presence of white people. It doesn't matter if it's Texas (whose black population was so stupid that they didn't even find out that slavery had ended until two years after the fact) or Georgia (a place with one of the lowest educational levels for blacks and whites, in the nation and one of the lowest in male faculty and salaries).

Then come the rumors that he killed a man and served time in Leavenworth or Louisiana. This was in addition to the rumor that he was in the army, went crazy and was committed to an asylum that he escaped from. And then finally in all these cases, he was "a fugitive from justice at the time he came to us." So what is the real issue here? The real issue is that this man had baggage and white people didn't give a shit when they found out that he had been in the army (meaning that he had successfully "served" them). They probably figured that if he killed someone, it must have been one of those "southern crackers" who called him a nigger. It doesn't matter what their justification was: none of this negative shit came to surface until he busted a cap in the asses of white folks.

This post-lynching rationalization and rumor-mongering is what the real America is about. Today in 2016 from their suburban living rooms they watch television, see black people getting gunned down in the streets by cops and immediately take the side of the police officer, automatically assuming that "the nigger must have done something wrong." That is why I concur with the statement by Karenga (1967) who once wrote that, "White doesn't represent a color; it represents a mentality that is anti-black." And this is why white racism in Europe and America is perpetual. White adults teach their children and their schools and media promote white supremacy.

The story is winding down:

> But all these stories came to nothing. Nothing was ever proved.
> Men debated and discussed these things a thousand times – who
> and what he had been, what he had done, where he had come from
> – and all of it came to nothing. No one knew the answer. But I
> think that I have found the answer. I think that I know from where
> he came.

Nothing was ever proved because white people didn't give a shit. They could have cared less because their cultural arrogance is always an impediment to getting at the truth. That's why Susan Smith could drown her baby boys and say 'a nigga stole the van and did it' and white cultural arrogance believes her. That's why Jesse Stuart in Milwaukee can knife his elderly wife coming out of a restaurant and plant a baseball cap, tell the cops 'a nigga did it' and the white cops believe it. That is why Jonathan Stuart in Boston can kill his pregnant wife, park the car in the projects, call the cops and say 'a nigga did it' and the cops lock up damn near all of the males in Roxbury. It's the same mentality: as long as the nigga is under the control of a white person (in this case living in the basement of the Sheppertons, they just don't care. And they continue to give short shrift to black initiative and guts.

The last paragraph of the short story is filled with color-coded racism:

> He came from darkness. He came out of the heart of darkness,
> from the dark heart of the secret and undiscovered South. He came
> by night, just as he passed by night. He was night's child and
> partner, a token of the other side of man's dark soul. A symbol of
> those things that pass by darkness and that still remain, a symbol of
> man's evil innocence. And the token of his mystery, a projection of
> his own unfathomed quality, a friend, a brother, and a mortal
> enemy, and unknown demon, two worlds together – a tiger and a
> child.

Although they don't know where he came from the assumption is that he "came from darkness." Why? Because darkness is negative and evil and since Prosser was a black man, he fit the racist mold. He came from the "dark heart of the undiscovered South." How is the South undiscovered? Is it just that the racists in the north don't want to claim it? And why is their heart "dark"? For the same reason that the word "blackheart" is negative: a "blackheart" is someone who is cruel, wicked or malevolent. Prosser is said to be a "night's child and partner" and "the other side of man's dark soul." Wolfe just keeps on piling it on, doesn't he? Somehow Prosser is all this negative while it is presumed that the white boys were his innocent victims.

In this final paragraph Wolfe also writes that Prosser was, "A symbol of those things that pass by darkness and that still remain, a symbol of man's evil innocence." All this because a black man got tired of taking the white man's bullshit, bullshit that the white man views as "par for the course" and nothing out of the ordinary. Racism, to them, is a human emotion that is perfectly understandable. Claiming Mexicans are lazy, that Japanese can't drive, that blacks are criminals or that Native Americans are drunks is all a part of white stereotype culture and many (if not most) of them accept it, lock, stock and barrel.

And the final sentence, quite long in fact, is aimed at putting a final thought into the mind of the reader. After inundating the mind with all of this "black equals negative" imagery, the story's final line reads, "And the token of his mystery, a projection of his own unfathomed quality, a friend, a brother, and a mortal enemy, and unknown demon, two worlds together – a tiger and a child."

Dick Prosser was black and he was a man, and this story refused to acknowledge either one. He was no tiger because a tiger is an animal and Dick Prosser was a human being. He was no child because he was a full grown man who knew what he was doing and had mastered a number of skills as the white youth pointed out. What Dick Prosser was, in plain terms, was a victim of racism. As are we all – both black and white.

"THE INVASION OF THE BODY SNATCHERS": AN ANTI-COMMUNISM MOVIE

The white man's fear of black people is intense and has a long tradition. But his fear of what he called "the Communist scare" was a national phenomenon that led to massive interrogations, what he called "blacklisting" and a plethora of other anti-communist tactics. Throughout the 1950s, a white boy senator named Joe McCarthy intimidated an entire nation into thinking that America was going to be taken over by "the communists." A clear-cut case of white-on-white crime.

As usual, creatures from another planet want to take over the world. So where do they come? The most war-like, brutal and kill-happy nation on the planet. What istheir plan? To morph from their seeds/pods into white people, infiltrate their ranks and take over. Not bad. Again, this goes back to the "Communist scare" that plagued America in the 1950s when the big concern was that "the commies" were coming and they were going to "radicalize" young people and there would be some kind of internal takeover. Sound familiar? It's the same fear these white people have today of middle easterners who are using the internet to "radicalize" white kids and turn them into suicidal terrorists.

According to Robey (2014),

> Don Siegel and producer Walter Wanger were quick off the mark in adapting Jack Finney's 1955 novel. They shot the film in under a month and for less than $400,000. It was intended as a B thriller, no more, no less: the many layers of political allegory which generations of viewers have since disinterred were quite some way from the makers' thoughts.

It was a propaganda film. The American cinema had already inundated audiences with the myth of the omnipotent white male adult and the irresistible white female. But this one was about alien beings who come to earth as pods and take over the lives of men, women, kids and young adults. In other words, instead of destroying white people, they duplicate them and make them even MORE sinister and unfeeling!:

> Of course, it's the very open-endedness of the film's subtext that gives it power. When a sleepy California town is overrun, first by the outbreak of a strange delusion that people have been replaced by doppelgangers, but then gradually by the doppelgangers themselves, the film is brilliantly placed, however unwittingly, to illustrate America's political paranoia from both ends. (Robey, 2014)

How is the movie open-ended just because it doesn't tell you what happens at the conclusion? You already know what happens: the white man wins, as usual! Even though the pods have been "discovered" and increasing numbers of white people have had their bodies taken over, the concept of "invasion" is one that only provides fodder for the white man to come to his senses at the last minute and come up with something. You don't have to show him doing it on the screen: the white supremacy system has been at work for a century convincing the American public that they are invincible and can overcome any and all odds.

The fear of communism is but a façade, in my view: the key is the belief that superior aliens would send in pods to take over the bodies of white people in a small hick town. Why not an urban area? Because they would have to replicate some black people and the superior technology probably warned them that white folks ain't gonna be picking up no giant pods and taking them home to the crib! White people and their "that's peculiar" approach to anything different, will venture forth and grab, touch, fuck *anything*, and the aliens probably knew that! The writers certainly did!

But the theme of this book*: long live the revolution*. Kudos to the aliens for having the nerve to see a planet this fucked up and still have the nerve to attack it. Here they have a planet that just got out of a world war, where the population in charge (whites) have just dropped two atomic bombs on their fellow human beings in Japan, and where the country is in an upheaval based on racism. And yet they see room where there can be a successful "invasion"?

RED DAWN: TWO FILMS, SAME PATRIOTIC THEME

The first time I saw "Red Dawn," I was impressed. Not so much with the predictable plot, but with the strategies employed by high school kids in fighting to defend their Midwestern, somewhat hickish community.

It starts off while many of them are in school and then they begin to look outside the window to see men parachuting all over the surrounding countryside, including on their school grounds. In typical fashion, the only black who is a part of the community is also the teacher, Mr. Teasdale (played by Frank McRae) and decides to "go outside and check it out." He gets unmercifully gunned down by the invaders and fear and hysteria sweep the school as the kids all try to make a run for it.

Red Dawn, 1984

The first version was incredible and the second one was a repetition with better acting. So let's do the initial flick, which starred Patrick Swayze and some other "brat pack" types. Just as Crispus Attucks, a black man, was the first man to die in the Revolutionary War, so it was with the 1984 edition of "Red Dawn." A black school teacher in a midwestern classroom (fat chance) with a room full of white kids spots some paratroopers landing in the field nearby.

Now instead of this nigga evacuating and heading to the storm shelters which we know were in existence, he goes to the window, adopts that "hmmm, that's peculiar" attitude that white folks always show in these kinds of movies, and assumes that all of those men who are parachuting into the field "must be off course." He then boldly takes his overweight black ass outside and immediately gets capped. The kids, watching from the safety of the classroom windows, start screaming and running in order to avoid the same fate as their teacher.

And that's how these young guys, who get picked up in a speedy pickup by their older brother (former star athlete at the school who has since graduated) comes by, swoops them up and off they head to the mountains where they hide, train themselves in guerilla warfare (another white fantasy) and begin going back to "take back" the town that they love.

The Cubans have landed and are led by Ron O'Neal (star of Super Fly) and have taken over the town. This guy, Colonel Bella, is torn because as the kids begin kicking ass he can relate because before he sold out he too was a revolutionary. But then, in order to whip up the patriotic frenzy akin to what you see at these college and pro football games when these white people lose their minds, the film turns sadistic. As reviewer Gregory Hood (2016) described the scene:

> Nonetheless, the Wolverines don't become a military rebellion until sightseeing Soviet troops accidentally run into them in the woods. In self-defense, the Americans are forced to kill them with bows and arrows and hunting rifles. In retaliation, the Soviets force American civilians to dig graves for the Red Army troops before executing them. Defiantly, the doomed men sing a startlingly off-key rendition of "America the Beautiful" before being gunned down by .50 caliber machine guns. (Hood, 2016)

Again, America is made out to be the victim. But even more insultingly, these trained, expert Russian soldiers are continually overcome and defeated by mere children. And America wonders why Putin and the Russians are constantly dogging out the country in real life. They (the Russians) see how they are portrayed in American movies, knowing full well that as screwed up as the Russian autocracy is, America is really no better when it comes to the final outcomes: they (the American government) just hides it better.

Referring to the communists as "reds" is why the movie is called "Red Dawn." The Russians are "on the rise" and headed inland. They have invaded America. But as the American version of all movies go, even the gooniest, most backward and youthful U.S. citizen is superior to the most advanced Russian soldier. Time and time again these kids make asses out of the invading Russian army, using patchwork weapons against sophisticated tanks, handguns and bombs.

So the Russians make if "personal" by not only invading the country but by taking out the relatives of the kids as well. Now the kids are REALLY pissed off:

> Arturo's and the Eckerts' father are both murdered, as the boys look on in horror. Jed tells the weeping group to stop crying, and is joined by Robert, who is ready for vengeance. The guerrilla campaign is about to begin. All of this happens extremely quickly and is essentially a setup to develop several classical Right-wing themes.(Hood, 2016).

These rookies all of a sudden become skilled in guerilla warfare. But the kidsd also become skilled politicians and begin making value judgments against the townspeople who are being passive and submissive and don't want to resist the Russian incursion.

Hood (2016) writes of the movie:

> The movie makes several clumsy but sincere efforts towards humanizing the enemy. Colonel Bella, always on the side of the insurgents in the past, is disgusted to find himself "a policeman" repressing a hostile population. At the end of the film, he disgustedly writes to his wife that he's done with the "revolution" and that he will resign and come home to her. He even lets Jed escape (though presumably to die in peace) rather than finishing him.(Hood, 2016).

To begin with, let us not get it twisted. As is the case today in 2017 when the political pundits keep trying to make it appear as if Russia and America hate each other's guts, there is an old saying: "Brothers may fight, but brothers will still be brothers." America and England made up following that ass whipping during the Revolutionary War. America kissed Germany's ass with the Marshall Plan following that war. These white people share something in common: whiteness! Russia and America are two white nations that both hate niggas! Don't you get it? There is racial unity which trumps ideological dissimilarities!

With that understood, let us know look at the preceding excerpt where it says, "The movie makes several clumsy but sincere efforts towards humanizing the enemy." And I offer that it is because "the enemy" is as white as the Russians are. Skin color (or colorlessness) is what they see. So ideology aside, you have white men fighting one another meaning that along racial lines, there is always a feeling of "humanity" because in their culture, all whites are human beings and the rest of humanity constitute mongrels of some kind.

The white kids are humanized and so are the Russian adults. That is because they are all white. The one black man in the entire movie (other than Bella who is played by Ron O'Neal) is an overweight school teacher who is made to look like a nosey asshole as he sees soldiers parachuting into the fields near the school yard and instead of having the kids go into the auditorium and hunker down, he takes his fat nosey ass outside and has the gall to ask, "Hey, you guys lost"? As a result of this ignorant question, the brutha is dehumanized with a bunch of bullets in his ass.

The Russians are therefore humanized in a number of ways. Hood (2016) points out that,

> Soviet soldiers play tourist, playfully mock each other, and ineptly
> try to translate American monuments and identify local animals.
> There's the occasional closeup to show that the Soviet soldiers are
> painfully young – as young as the Wolverines who are butchering
> them. One begs Daryl to tell him his name before he's executed, so
> he doesn't die alone. Another cries to God for help as he is dying,
> and turns away when Jed places a pistol to his head, too young and
> scared to face the reality of death. (Hood, 2016).

So even though it is war, the white man is shown having the full range of emotional content. Both of the groups represent killers and the kids learn quickly the art and science of guerilla warfare. The justification for this quick lesson is that "this is our home" and the mountains that they are hiding in and the forests that they are using for cover are places where they often frequented since they were born and raised there.

And this brings us to the inter-generational nature of the leadership that these kids almost instinctively learn:

> Matt and Jed's survival and leadership role is enabled by the
> training they received from their father. Their father named Jed
> after frontiersman Jed Smith and taught them to hunt and survive
> in the woods. When they encounter him in the concentration camp,
> he tells them that he was hard on them growing up, "but you know
> why now." This can only be a reference to giving the boys rough
> training in survivalism, teaching them to "man up" in difficult
> situations, and filling their heads with paranoia about a dangerous
> world. Of course, just because you are paranoid doesn't mean that
> there isn't someone there out to get you. (Hood, 2016).

So Jed is named after a frontiersman and is taught to hunt by his father. That is how the tradition continues. His father apparently anticipated this kind of problem and tells his kid that he now knows why he was taught how to hunt. "Red Dawn" is revolutionary in the since that it shows young people as military killers, as guerilla fighters. But what they were doing was not the revolutionary aspect of the movie in my view: what they were undertaking was "counter-revolutionary" activity – they were defending the United States against a force that was working toward changing the status quo!

As for race (or the lack of it), Hood (2016) writes the following:

> *Red Dawn* does not contain many non-white faces, which has led
> to the accusations of racism, but the still American West of the
> 1980s didn't contain many either. With a (presumably) Mexican-
> American father executed by the Reds, a black teacher serving as
> the Crispus Attucks of the occupation, the son of the martyred

> Mexican a Wolverine who dies at the side of Lt. Col. Tanner, and
> the Cuban occupiers portrayed sympathetically, it's hard to argue
> that Milius was being deliberately racist. (Hood, 2016).

You see what happens when white reviewers attempt to deal with racial issues. Hood writes that because of the examples he's pointed out that, "it's hard to argue that Milius was being deliberately racist." This falls back to that "unconscious racist," "unintentional bias" bullshit that society is being force-fed to absolve white folks of their guilty. You can therefore be a racist and not really mean it. What kind of sick bullshit is that?

In order to get those roles you have to audition. There is a role for a teacher, Mr. Teasdale (played by Frank McRae). So into the audition walks this overweight brutha who has done a few movies before. He reads the script and the director and others decide to make him the perfect sucka for the opening scene. Why? Because that's the last nigga you're going to see for a long time, that's why. And it is Teasdale's stupidity that opens the door for the kids to begin fleeing the scene, some getting killed, and the main actors jumping into the back of a pickup truck and making their escape. All that is based on a racist decision.

The choice of location also absolves the director and writers of having to have a diverse cast. Although Ron O'Neal played Priest in the movie "SuperFly," he plays Colonel Ernesto Bella, obviously a Cuban of some kind. His race is therefore nullified. Another racist decision because is there any doubt that darker skinned bruthas auditioned for that role?

To make the racial analysis even worse, Hood further opines that, "The only reference to racial genocide comes from a Russian colonel, who argues that the Americans must all be killed like animals, just like "in Afghanistan." How is that about "race"? Afghanistani's are brown skinned so there is no way that these white kids would be compared with that part of the world other than the fact that the Afghans were resisting America in the same way that the Americans were now resisting the Russians. That is not about race: that is about geopolitical advantage and ideology!

In the end Hood concludes what I have pointed out, but even in his agreement there is blatant error. Check it out:

> The film is of course institutionally racist because it shows a
> mostly white America filled with mostly noble white people
> fighting in defense of their mostly white families. A progressive
> film would have showed them greeting the Cubans and
> Nicaraguans as liberators and begging their forgiveness for
> slavery, oppression of the Indians and the existence of the United
> Fruit Company. (Hood, 2016).

And herein lies another teaching point for you, the reader. Take note that Hood makes an important observation when he notes of the institutional racism that it, "shows a mostly white America filled with mostly noble white people fighting in defense of their mostly white families." There is nothing wrong with that and it's not necessary racist in itself. What is racist is why those communities are all-white, why their school is lily-white but the teacher is Black and never gets harassed, why there are no black people in the movie other than Mr. Teasdale, and why more audience members are willing to accept this drivel without raising the points that Hood and I just did.

The kids hold off the would-be invaders – young white boy hicks overcoming trained soldiers, akin to the white nationalism that can be seen in "Invasion USA." The real army then comes in and mops up the invaders and the "Red dawn" is vanquished. "Red," by the way, is the nickname these white people gave to Communists. So it may have been a dawning of a Communist invasion, but by the time they finished getting their asses kicked, it was the setting of the white nationalist American sun.

Red Dawn, 2012

If North Korea and America every go to war in the real world, I am pretty sure that this movie – and other movies that tend to castigate North Korea – will be a part of the reason why. These white people in Hollywood (read: Jews) continue to pump out this new version of "cowboys and Indians" with the cowboys being the white American military and today's "Indian" being any country of color. In this movie that country, the one that invades America's shore, hails from North Korea.

The late Roger Ebert's website offers the following introduction:

> "Red Dawn" opens with a hard-fought high school football game,
> the day before Spokane, Wash. is interrupted by the thud of bombs.
> The young gridiron stars of the Wolverines race outside to see
> enemy aircraft flying overhead in formation, dropping paratroopers
> from the skies. (Ebert, 2012).

So in the original movie the kids were in school and the invaders landed in a nearby field. In this one the football game is the key and paratroopers are spotted dropping in. In both cases we see trained military men who had to be engaged in months, if not years, of planning for this invasion, dropping into crowded public areas and in doing so, spreading chaos and havoc. There is nothing secret about what they are doing and it looks totally helter-skelter. This is the white Americans version of what an invasion would be like: once again, putting down and insulting their enemies (this time Koreans) while inferior whites (school kids) somehow acquire guerilla warfare skills to take out the "gooks" (ala Vietnam?).

Even Roger Ebert's analysts could see the fallacy in both movies:

> If you're wondering how North Korea (population 25 million) can raise enough invaders to attack the Unites States (population 315 million), it may help to understand that the original screenplay for this remake named the invaders as Chinese. After principal photography was completed on this film three years ago and its studio (MGM) went belly-up, the enemy identity was changed to North Korea by reshooting several scenes, redubbing lots of dialogue and using digital adjustment to change the looks of flags, uniforms and insignia on trucks and tanks. Did this involve a change in ideology in Hollywood? Not really. A marketing genius figured out that China is one of the biggest markets for American movie exports, and North Korea generates unimpressive box-office bucks for Yank product, as the trade papers like to word it. (Ebert, 2012)/

One point was omitted from the previous political analysis: Hollywood is run by Jews, and the more havoc and division they can spread by bringing in other nations the less attention can be placed on how Jews in Israel are abusing and killing off the Palestinians.

A partial truth can be found where it is noted that, "A marketing genius figured out that China is one of the biggest markets for American movie exports, and North Korea generates unimpressive box-office bucks for Yank product, as the trade papers like to word it." The reviewer forgot to mention that China despises North Korea and sides with America against them. In the first movie another nation that America had issues with, Cuba, was the bad guy. Both countries are communist, hence the use of the term "red."

The red star of China is flashed and excerpts of Hillary Clinton are shown then, onto the screen flashes, "Red Dawn."

The movie's premise is jejune and simplistic. As Ebert (2012) writes, "This is an alarming sight, but not to worry: The movie reassures us that an invasion by communist North Korea can be vanquished by the members of the team and their girlfriends, using mostly automatic weapons stolen from the North Koreans themselves." This is all said tong-in-cheek, but of course this is being fed to American audiences who, blinded by a patriotic and mythical belief that America is unbeatable, will easily gobble up this drivel in the same way they believe that there is no alien force that can defeat Earth (if led by white people and Jews) and no entity that can defeat their nearly all-white legions of super heroes, from the Justice League to the Avengers.

At least this second installment offered some semblance of an explanation as to how young kids got military training. In this sequel the football team is headed by the star player, Matt, who is the younger brother of Jed, who just so happens to be a Marine returning home from active duty. In fact as the movie opens, he's sitting in his truck outside of the fence watching the game. He then walks into the stadium and watches his team, the Wolverines, play. His brother is the quarterback, and they lose the game. Jed walks away and everyone iss disappointed.

And so along with Matt's girlfriend, who just so happens to be a cheerleader and another girl who falls for Jed, this serves as the core of the kiddies who are going to teach the invading army a lesson or two. All white-created revolutionary movies contain an underlying theme: No matter how many bombs, bullets or beast-like men are invading or about to the invaded, the white man always has time to stick his tongue down some woman's throat and, where time allows, get an erection. In other words, the

movie is another attempt to show "white power" in the face of quashing attempted revolutionary takeovers by outsiders. But Ebert (2012) does raise some important questions:

> The story's time frame is confusingly murky. How long does it take the North Koreans to land, import their heavy weapons and vehicles, enlist local traitors and start running things? What is their game plan? Is this a national invasion? How do they plan petrol deliveries? We're unclear about what's happening in the rest of the United States. (Ebert, 2012).

These are all pertinent questions, but they are rooted in the reality of revolution and war. These movies are propaganda pieces, and both of the presentations of "Red Dawn" are about embellishing on the fighting skills of all Americans (even teenagers) and how they would easily use guerilla warfare (that they are not trained in) to defeat lifelong soldiers, first from Cuba and then from North Korea. Coincidentally in real life, American hates both countries.

The two movies do share something in common. Just as the lone black in the first movie, Mr. Teasedale, got a cap busted in his ass after wandering outside to "see what's going on" as he watches hundreds of paratroopers landing in a field, there is also a token black in the second installment. He's a kid named Danny Jackson. And he plays a pivotal role: after one of their raids and the kids all make their mistake, it seems that it's Danny who has been "tagged" with a tracking transmitter and the Russians are homing in on them. Just like Teasedale was the Crispus Attucks of the first movie, Danny sacrifices himself by staying behind so that the others might live. This is what Black Panther Party founder Huey Newton would have called "revolutionary suicide."

The revolutionary spirit/guerilla warfare instincts of the kids in both versions of "Red Dawn" are worthy of paying attention to, just like the workings of the "dirty cops" in "Triple 9.' As Ebert (2012) put it,

> They're also gifted strategists, instinctively occupying the high ground and spraying bullets down upon the hapless enemy forces who are often conveniently lined up in the street below. They achieve all of these things with remarkably little dialogue; mostly they just shout exhortations at one another and eavesdrop on speeches to the population by the enemy leader, Capt. Cho (Will Yun Lee). (Ebert, 2012)

So even young upstarts can overpower a trained military force. This is what you have to be able to want to do in order to wage a revolution – or prevent one from taking place. But America makes a major mistake: they over-estimate their own worth and continue to under-estimate their opposition. Just like they did in the case of Vladimir Putin and Russia.

Instead, all you get is patriotic bullshit and victory under unreal circumstances:

> I'm not sure I saw any Wolverines actually killed — at least no major characters. I'm sure I must have seen countless North Koreans mowed down, but given the movie's PG-13 rating, the carnage is far from graphic. A closing scene, rousingly patriotic, takes place back on the football field. I think I'm beginning to understand why the Chinese were not reckoned to be a prime market for this film. (Ebert, 2012),

And so it goes with both installments of the movie "Red Dawn." Although some 28 years apart, what they show in combination is that the pro-American belief still lingers and people of color, whether invading from Cuba or from North Korea, don't have a chance against the mighty white man.

Or the white teenager.

BADGE 373: PUERTO RICO LIBRE!

This movie is very interesting because it provides the revolutionary vanguard, the Puerto Rican bruthas in the streets of New York, a number of opportunities to voice anti-American sentiments by pinpointing the plethora of atrocities that the U.S. has imposed on the island of Puerto Rico and its people.

The movie was not widely viewed, but its revolutionary bent is probably the reason why. It was released in 1973, the same year that the overwhelming majority of "blaxploitation" movies were released (e.g., "Hell Up in Harlem," Scream, Blacula,Scream," "Slaughter's Big Rip-Off," "The Mack," "Gordon's War," "Black Caesar," to name but a few). "Badge 373" was not a black movie, per se, but it featured brown men (Puerto Ricans are black in my view) and they were standing tall against the racist police department. The lead character was admittedly a racist:

> Eddie Ryan (Robert Duvall), a tough, no-nonsense, abrasive and racist Irish NYPD cop, has to turn in his badge after scuffling with a Puerto Rican suspect who then falls to his death from a rooftop, but that doesn't stop him from heading out on a one-man crusade to find out who killed his partner of three years, Gigi Caputo (Louis Cosentino), all the while neglecting his new live-in girlfriend, Maureen (Verna Bloom). Ryan's search leads him to Puerto Rican drug kingpin Sweet Willie (Henry Darrow), and a shipment of guns for Puerto Rican *independenistas*. (Wikipedia, 2016; Ebert, 1973).

In real life this guy, Eddie Ryan, was a kind of cult hero. He was one of those racist supercops that white folks like so much. The kind who goes into his favorite pub and brags to his pals about all the "niggers" he "tuned up" or how many "black bitches" he copped a feel on. They're all over the place. Omaha had a bunch of them back in the day, and the older blacks remember them well. One of them, Jimmy Wilson, Sr., would walk into a black club, take off his holster and challenge any black man to take a swing. Of course, the bruthas could have kicked his ass, but they know what would happen if they beat up a cop. So this part of the movie is a classic case of art imitating life – and vice versa.

And that "scuffle" with the Puerto Rican that is described above was a little bit more than that. The fact is, the Puerto Rican brother was running upstairs and Ryan could have let him go. But he was bent on teaching this kid a lesson and tracked him down. Then, after trapping him atop a roof, the kid still tried to run and Ryan stood there as the kid fell. It was Ryan's fault and the street was full of cops and other witnesses. Nobody did a damn thing.

As for his partner, he was this Italian guy. The Italians treated black people as bad as the Jews and the Irish did. Ryan uses the death of his partner, Gee Gee, to go after whomever he think did it. For starters, he (Ryan) should have never been allowed to work that case – it was personal. But these are white boys and the targets are going to be young people of color. So these assholes in blue bend the rules and look the other way in the name of justice, which is just another word for "vengeance."

Now the guns are the real story. These Puerto Rican bruthas aren't bullshittin'. They are tired of the United States messing with their native country and want to do something about it. One good thing about this movie is that the arguments that these young men make are sound and historically accurate. But this drunk asshole cop only sees one thing: brown skin. The key is that these bruthas are out to ship $3 million worth of machine guns to Puerto Rico so that they can begin their revolution. And that is why this movie, the lesser known of the five mentioned in this book, is included.

In a scene that lasts far too long, Ryan is leaving a bar and the Puerto Ricans are waiting on him. There must be at least twenty of them and they want blood. Somehow, this slow white man manages to escape them and the chase is on. Down the streets the flee until Ryan commandeers a metro bus, throws the driver out on the street and then, with passengers still onboard, takes off as the Puerto Ricans jump in their cars and chase this bus all over the streets of New York. A more unrealistic scene you will rarely see.

Remember that Ryan has been suspended following the death of that Puerto Rican who "fell" off a roof. But he tells his chief, "I'm still a cop – badge or no badge." And he lives up to that pledge. He wants to go after the gang that he learns was behind the death of Gee-Gee. Now we're back on the bus speeding through the streets. Eventually the bus crashes into the plate glass window of store after the Puerto Ricans shoot out the tires of the bus.

The Puerto Ricans grab Ryan from the bus and are stomping the hell out of him until the head gang leader, Ruben, calls them off. As police sirens are heard, the gang runs off. In the next scene is Ryan in a hospital bed as his girlfriend enters with flowers. He needs some rest and relaxation. They venture to a cabin he owned and begin playing house. One of his arms is in a cast, but that doesn't stop him from having target practice every day, using trees for targets. He's also created a nice sawed-off shotgun as the woman watches him. She doesn't want him to return to the city but this white man is bent on revenge. The fact that the people he's chasing are brown-skinned Puerto Ricans and he's a racist provides even more incentive.

Ryan returns to the city and is surveilling a Puerto Rican meeting after following a car to where the meeting is being held. The sign says Despierta Boricua – Defiende Lo Tuyo." The speaker is the gang leader, Ruben Garcia sporting a large Afro.

> "We didn't ask to come here," he shouts. "Every time my mother
> is hassled at the welfare office I tell her to tell them 'we didn't ask
> to come to this madness called the United States.' They invaded
> our country, grabbed our land right from under us and then forced

us to come here by the hundreds of thousands, by the millions, to serve as cheap sources of labor in their garment centers where we sew the clothes that we can't even afford to wear!"

After much applause, Ruben continues:

"We came here as farmers, many of us, poor – but proud. And we ended up as porters, we ended up as dish washers, we ended up as messenger boys, we ended up as 45 year old errand boys and door men. I mean, can you dig that? Brown kings and queens with a proud past holding some doors open and forcing themselves to smile. What has American imperialism done for the island, baby? What it has done is it has turned our island into a combination whore house, a combination gambling casino and dope drop …"

He continues:

"And the puppet governors have stood by while thirteen percent of the best farmland in Puerto Rico is made into military bases. The puppet governors stood by while they destroyed our culture and substituted it by telling our children that to look as pale and as sick as they are is hipper and healthier than having the color of the sun. American businessmen pay one third of what they pay here in the United States, yet the workers in Puerto Rico have to pay twenty-five percent more for the junk surplus that they throw at Puerto Rico. Naw, hell naw. We're not going for it any more. And we'll do whatever is necessary to free our island from the shackles of American imperialism. We'll do whatever is necessary. And if we can't rap about it, then we're going to shoot our way to it. We've got to march from New York to San Juan, let us march from Chicago to Maya West. Let us march toward the free land of our ancestors. Viva Lucha! Free Puerto Rico! … "

Ryan is following someone through the crowd and at the end of the speech commends him to two other white men who also agree that the kid is a good speaker. Ryan and two men enter a fantastic large home of William Salazar. They shake hands and Salazar has checked Ryan out. Ryan is seated. He pours Ryan a Scotch, neet.

They talk about a revolution without enough guns. Ryan tells him t get to the point. Salarzar says he is in the business of survival, that he will make much more money and then offers Ryan a job. "Your partner passed away," he tells Ryan. They are talking about a shipment of guns to Puerto Rico – three million dollars worth. Ryan jumps out of a window and leaves the scene. Ryan is in the water and gets rescued. He calls Maureen to bring him some dry clothes.

Salazar meets with Ruben, the latter sporting a machine gun, the former a brief case filled with money. They are paying Salazar for the guns to send back for a revolution. Salazar spills his guts about how he got to America. His mother died of cancer and his brother died also. His father sold books, sold the land "and took a trip to New York." When Ruben asks him what happened to his father, Salazar says, "He was a dreamer. The world always kills a dreamer." (NOTE: Interesting. This movie was released five years after the assassination of the ultimate "dreamer," Dr. Martin Luther King, Jr.).

The guns are being shipped. "They'll be coming in Gate 3," the truck driver tells Salazar and Ruben. He asks Ruben for the machine gun to have as a souvenir. Ruben gives it to him and then hands him the clip. Salazar now has the gun. Ryan and Maureen are waiting outside of the police station. They follow one of the cops, the one named Diaz who Ryan says killed Gee-Gee. Maureen stops the car, jumps out, and is immediately gunned down. Ryan cries over her body, hand still in a cast.

Trucks filled with guns are leaving Salazar's house. Ryan has somehow managed to get to the house. He sits in the kitchen. "Hey spic," he says. It's Diaz house. He pushes around Diaz and his wife and has both at gunpoint. "Ya finally made it, eh Diaz? A fine little house!" Ryan yells as he throws all the furnishings off the kitchen table. He continues tearing up the kitchen. He's yelling about the kids that Gee-Gee had who were in school. Diaz says he didn't kill Ryan's partner but blames it on the Puerto Rican gang.He forces Diaz down on the floor and makes him crawl backwards in his tidy whiteys and t-shirt to the window. He orders the wife to handcuff Diaz and herself to the radiator pipe.

"Where is Sweet William delivering those fuckin' guns?" he asks Diaz at gunpoint. Ryan calls the cop shop and tells them the ship that the guns are going out on. He tells Eddie that he can have the guns and the bust, "But I want Sweet William." Eddie hangs up before Ryan can finish.

Ryan heads to Lancaster, Pennsylvania and subdues a security guard on the dock. The trucks with the guns have arrived. Ryan hides around the corner. A guard walks up the ryan subdues him, takes his gun and walks on. The trucks back in to the loading dock near the ship. Cop sirens blare and are on the way. The lading begins. Sweet William, Ruben and Salazar are watching. Ryan walks up on them and mercilessly shoots down Ruben. They all run. Salazar makes a run for it after grabbing the machine gun that Ruben gave him earlier. The men on the ship want to pll away as Salazar orders them back, shooting one. The cops are now pulling up.

Sweet William is being arrested by the cops.Ryan is after Salazar; "You spic son of a bitch!" Scanlon is trying to reach emergency services. He wants shotguns and bullet proof vests. Ryan is still chasing Salazar. "Come on Ryan – I'm ready for you!" he shouts. "I'm waiting!" Ryan scales the stairs where Salazar is located. Higher and higer they go. The cop orders the others to hold their fire as they watch the two men. "Eddie come on down," the head cop orders.

"Come on you useless pendejos. I own you all!" Salazar shouts. The shootout ends. The revolution is thwarted.

INVASION USA

This 1985 movie was a distortion of revolutionary planning and strategy. It was clumsy and so were the guys who were "invading" the United States. Actually, it was one man – Chuck Norris (Matt Hunter – what a coincidence) against some unorganized thugs in one part of the United States – Florida, of all places. Oh – they get him out of retirement as if he is the only man in Florida with skill (and balls) enough to stop the violence that has "invaded" the Sunshine State.

Roger Ebert sums it up nicely:

> The movie is about an invasion of the United States by several boatloads of vicious killers, who come from somewhere (Cuba, maybe?) and leave their amphibious vehicles on the beach. They pile into a caravan of rented trucks and vans and spread out across Florida, using grenades, machineguns and bazookas to destroy anything that looks remotely like a wholesome American image. Examples: School buses full of kids, shopping malls, church services and even suburban families decorating\ Christmas trees while singing "Hark! The Herald Angels Sing!" (Ebert, 1985)

The whole movie was a white nationalist promotion. What Ebert refers to as the attempt to "destroy anything that looks remotely like a wholesome American image" translates to mean a WHITE cultural image, which is why quasi-religious symbols like Christmas trees, singing choirs and church services are included. But that is just a reviewer's assessment. My research goes much deeper. The story was actually written by Chuck's brother Aaron, and some Jew named James Bruner. From that, the screenplay was written by Bruner and Chuck. Three white nationalists with a bone to pick with anything not American (or white).

It gets deeper. This guy Bruner appears to be a Chuck Norris flunky. He has written movies like "Missing in Action (1984), "The Delta Force" (1986), along with "Braddock: Missing in Action III" and "Behind Enemy Lines." All of these movies promote the white military man who can almost single handedly overcome any adversary, and in most cases, these adversaries are people of color. As for "Invasion USA," Ebert (1985) asks and answers, "Who are they? Their leader, named Rostov, sometimes seems Russian, usually sounds American. His followers are sometimes Oriental, sometimes Latino, usually anonymous." The point that Ebert misses is that they are not anonymous because they represent "the other" – it's white man versus the "outsider." The point being made is crystal clear.

The Movie Bastard reviewer website seemed as critical of the movie as I have been. At one point it is observed that,

> A lot of it doesn't make perfect sense I'll admit. Like how Chuck knows where each of the terrorist cells are located. Or why he drives down one street so slow that it allows a procession of pimps, hookers, bikers, meth-heads and other low-lifers to give him lip. But none of this really springs to mind in any meaningful way whilst watching (or should I say Experiencing) this film. (The Movie Bastard, 2013).

But as is usually the case, the white reviewers either don't see or totally overlook the racist elements of even the most simple scenes. White nationalism has been able to perpetuate itself because of the details, not so much the obvious symbols. Many of the latter have been attacked, protested against and as a result, well hidden over the centuries. But the subtle nuances, especially when the issue has to do with "white power" is what must be analyzed and understood.

The overriding racist theme is that one white man is the equivalent of a hundred revolutionary invaders. From that general theme stem a number of others, including the time of the year (December – the "holiday season"), the callousness of the invaders (attempting to blow up a school bus filled with young children), and the fight scenes where Norris literally destroys trained guerillas although at the outset of the movie is is brought out of retirement for this "mission." This fact in and of itself is an insult that implies that the existing police force and National Guard cannot get the job done. But one white man can.

So we have another invasion that is pawned off as just that, falls short of a revolution -– an *attempted* overthrow. But since it was unsuccessful, it becomes diminished to a mere "revolt." Again, The Movie Bastard (2013) adds some interesting sentiments:

> An honest complaint would be that there isn't much blood. Nor are there any eagle cries when he disappears like Batman every now and then. There are plenty of explosions however, and some brief nudity. Some parts are genuinely well done too, such as the final siege with the tanks, the "roll-out" moment with the trucks as the

invasion begins, and the decimation of American small-town
suburban Christmas ...

Tanks. Trucks, Rocket-Propelled Grenades. These are useless in a Chuck Norris film – unless HE is using them. The "invasion" that is attempted is awkward and poorly planned, akin to the Puerto Rican attempt in "Badge 373." These invaders come in from Florida and seem to think that attacking neighborhood homes and blowing up Christmas ornaments is the way to take over America. Chuck Norris literally takes out the revolutionary attempt by himself.

Pure nationalism and racism.

"RAMPAGE," "RAMPAGE: CAPITAL PUNISHMENT" and "RAMPAGE": – A TRULY REVOLUTIONARY TRILOGY OF MOVIES

This trilogy of movies contains a whole lot of killing, and as the movies progress, the attacker becomes increasingly political. I will address the content of each movie for its "revolutionary" content because each tells a story about the motivations behind this man's anti-governmental posturing.

In the first one, released in 2009, Bill Williamson is a young man in Tenderville, Oregon and he's living with his parents. He's got some anger management issues and it appears that no one, from the man at the local fast food store to regular people, will cut him a break. Unbeknownst to his parents, who are trying to get him to move out of their basement and perhaps go to college, Bill has a stash of weapons in his room and is skilled at building bombs and other types of weaponry. He has even manufactured a bullet proof black suit of armor that he apparently plans on wearing at a future date.

The second installment, "Rampage: Capital Punishment," follows his execution of all those people in Tenderville. He is now out spending the money that he stole from a bank he robbed at the end of the first rampage and heads to Washington, DC, where he comes across a television station. He enters and takes it over and has special hatred for the station's owner, Chip Parker. More on this later in the analysis.

In the third movie, "Rampage: President Down," Bill remains in Washington and uses his sniper skills to murder the president. More on each of these movies follows, with emphasis on the "revolutionary orientation" of Bill's thought process, comments and actions.

<u>Rampage (2009)</u>

Bill Williamson is a loser who works as a mechanic. He lives in his parents' basement and watches way too much television, listens to the radio and the stuff he hears is totally pissing him off. The key to the stuff he listens to is voiced on a video by a guy named Evan who Bill listens to regularly. At one point Evan says, "We need someone who will take some positive action." And that is what stuck, when added to information about the growing world population and the effect it's going to have on the American way of life.

The following day Bill goes through his usual routine before heading to work. He works out on his weights downstairs and the heavy bag with his boxing gloves. He goes upstairs to have breakfast with his parents and they continue to bug him about getting his life together. He tells them that he doesn't have the money to move out, but that he will fill out some applications for college. And they buy it for the time being.

At work Bill asks for a raise arguing that he is doing most of the work on the cars but the boss dismisses him. At home in the basement, Bill is busy at work, as the movie overview informs us:

> Back at home, Bill prints out fake money and then constructs a suit
> of AR-500 steel body armor, complete with a ballistic helmet and a
> paintball mask. Armed with two submachine guns, two
> semiautomatic pistols, and two knives, he heads into the center of
> town. First, he incapacitates the police by car-bombing their
> headquarters with a remote-controlled, bomb-loaded van
> (Wikipedia, 2016).

This guy had plenty of ammunition, clips of bullets, an Uzi and even a machete. The day then comes when he decides to make his move. He gets into his multi-colored Caprice Classic and heads to the downtown area. He puts on his helmet and then enters a van that he has stolen and loaded down with gasoline. By remote control he directs it into the police station, crashing it through. The station blows up and catches fire. It is at this time that the following takes place:

> He then walks through the streets, shooting people at random with
> the submachine guns, and stops to taunt and later kill the coffee
> shop owner. Two police officers open fire on him, but Bill's armor
> blocks the bullets and he kills both officers. He goes into a salon
> filled with several hiding women and takes off his mask in order to
> get a drink before leaving without shooting anyone, but then
> returns after realizing he revealed his identity to the salon
> occupants, all of whom he kills.(Wikipedia, 2016).

There is no explanation other than as the movie begins he rants about there being too many people in the world and that they're going to eat all the food and leave people like him with nothing. This is not a new argument but has been made over the centuries by white people who promote eugenics. One of the most popular of these was a man named Paul Erlich who wrote a book called The Population Bomb. One gets the feeling that the writer and director of these "Rampage" movies, some guy named Uwe Boll, feels the same way. He's a German who made one of my favorite movies, "Assault on Wall Street" where, as in the "Rampage" series, a man becomes frustrated and heads to the corporate offices and starts killing people – and gets away with it.

At any rate, "Rampage" continues:

> Bill goes unnoticed into a bingo parlor, orders a sandwich, harasses the host, and leaves without shooting anyone, believing the elderly patrons are already close enough to dying. He then enters a local bank, killing the security guard before shooting some of the employees and customers who attempt to subdue him. He proceeds to rob the bank, forcing the manager to empty a safe full of money into a plastic trash bag. Outside the bank, he secretly switches the money he stole with his fake money and burns the bag in a trash can, shouting that money is worthless and causes the problems of the world. (Wikipedia, 2016).

The "fake money" is money that he made in his basement courtesy of a photocopying machine. So this was all part of his plan. For anyone watching this movie to write Bill off as insane is ludicrous; this was premeditated, well planned and quite frankly it was an expensive undertaking. His points are being made at the expense of the people he paid, the institution he robbed and his statements about how "worthless" money is (while making sure that he saved plenty of the real money for himself). In fact, while robbing the bank he shoots one woman at the teller's window for having the nerve to "defend" the banking institution.

There is a scene that the review omitted that is most worthy of mention. At one point after killing scores of people, Bill enters a bingo parlor filled with older people who are focused on the bingo numbers. He walks around and they seem not to notice him. He goes to the front of the room and sits down after ordering a sandwich and some tea. After scarfing down his food and drink, Bill gets back up, looks around and walks out of the place. One wonders why he spared all of these elderly people. Some might say that he believed that they were near death anyway. But using logic, they were people who had been a part of the problem that Bill has outlined and had lived a long enough time to support the system Bill hates by way of their tax payments.

At any rate, Bill is a long way from being done:

> After killing a restaurant waitress who had previously agitated him,
> Bill calls Evan, who is in a forest nearby expecting him for a
> *mano-a-mano* paintball competition. Bill drives to the forest and is
> pursued by several police officers, led by Sheriff Melvoy. Bill kills
> most of the officers with explosives and flees into the forest,
> pursued by Melvoy, the only surviving policeman. When he
> arrives at the forest, Bill ambushes Melvoy, stabbing him and
> leaving him to die. Finding Evan, Bill immobilizes him with a stun
> gun and then places one of his pistols in Evan's hand, shooting him
> in the head to give the illusion of suicide. Bill puts the armor suit
> and weapons on Evan's corpse, leaves the forest, and burns
> remaining evidence in a barrel. (Wikipedia, 2016).

Evan is the talk show host who was on television agitating Bill by spewing forth a number of radical ideas. Time and time again Bill watched the show and each time he became more irate. Therefore as part of his plan, he located Evan, tazes him, and the puts his gun in Evans hand. As stated he dresses Evan up in his armored suit and therefore it looks like Evan committed the mass murders.

Moving on:

> Bill then returns home before his parents arrive with horror stories
> about the killings in town. While they are conversing in front of
> the television, news stations report that they have identified the
> killer as Evan, and that at least 93 people have been killed in the
> rampage. In his room, while packing his belongings and the stolen
> bank money, Bill hears a local television news report that police
> have arrested Evan's father, an activist during the Vietnam War
> era, who is accusing Bill of the crime and claiming the innocence
> of his son. The story concludes with a home video of Bill
> announcing his departure on a personal quest to unknown
> whereabouts, to further reduce the world's population. A text
> indicates Bill had disappeared from that point on, and two years
> later, his video recording found its way onto the Internet.

This is a truly revolutionary film, the first of three. They follow the trend of Uwe Boll's movies. In "Assault on Wall Street," a man gets tired of the system and he cannot afford his wife's increasing medical payments. When she dies, he snaps, loads up and gets his revenge. These themes are revolutionary because they directly confront the system. And remember that a "revolt" is an unsuccessful attempt to overthrow a system. A revolution is successful, and in these three movies Bill achieves his goal against the system

Rampage: Capital Punishment (2014)

It's called "capital punishment" because that is the next place where Bill heads – the nation's capital, and he takes over a television station and the killing spree continues. It's been a couple of years since Bill murdered over one hundred people in Tenderville, viewed as the largest mass killing spree in U.S. history. He continues his rants about population control. It's time for another killing spree. He also continues listening to his videotape of the now deceased Evan.

He works out in his new apartment while listening to Evan's rant. "Drones dropping bombs on little kids, plundering the Third World. The only way we can affect these lives is by taking them away. Get eleted? Get elected into what? Asange and snowden are prophets of our time." In his own tape Bill also talks about African leaders who exploit their own people. In my view his commitment to revolution has expanded from his small town (which he took out) to an entire worldview. Hence, his visit to Washington, DC, the center of the place where Bill believes all the problems begin.

As explained,

> Bill uses the stolen money to finance yet another killing spree,
> purchasing a number of weapons, including two fully automatic,
> military-grade M4 carbines, and constructing homemade
> explosives. After making final preparations for the killing spree,
> Bill shaves his head clean, dons his suit of body armor, and sets the
> interior of his house on fire. He drives to an alleyway and uses its
> cover to shoot several random pedestrians undetected, before
> trying to enter a bingo hall, only to leave after finding it is closed.
> (Wikipedia, 2016).

Bill is on his way to killing spree number two. He heads to a television station in DC where he blows up his car and enters the building. He shoots the security guard and several employees and then takes people hostage, including the news anchorman Chip Parker. He takes them into the basement at gunpoint. The overview continues:

> He kills one of the hostages when he disregards one of his orders.
> Bill later gives Chip a disc and instructs him to go upstairs and air
> the contents of the disc nationwide, then return with a camera crew
> so they could do a live interview with him. Chip agrees and leaves
> the basement, where he relays his instructions to the responding
> police officers. However, while trying to air the disc, he
> accidentally slips and breaks it. He returns to the basement and
> tells Bill what had happened, and an agitated Bill gives him a
> duplicate of the disc.(Wikipedia, 2016).

While Chip is gone Bill gets into a beef with one of the hostages because he doesn't like her style. So he shoots her. After that he's confronted by another hostage who foolishly tells him that she is the sister of one of the people that he killed in Tenderville. So what does Bill do? After the woman says that she plans to kill him, he picks out a male hostage and orders him to beat the shit out of her, which he does.

After that,

> Eventually, the contents of the disc are aired on live television; in it, Bill rants in a video recording about how the current system is flawed and that the U.S. government is manipulating American citizens and events for the sake of wealth. The video ends with Bill appealing to the American people to retaliate violently against politicians and the wealthy in order to restore society. Meanwhile, the officers manage to contact Bill's father with the intention of using him to appeal to Bill. (Wikipedia, 2016).

What was described above as a "rant" was no rant if you understand social dynamics. Everything that Bill was saying about the system and its abuses was right on target. He was pissed off at the government for it's on-going abuse of all people, but of course he didn't care about racial issues. After all, he's white and that means that his first commitment is to his whiteness

> Chip returns to the basement with a camera crew, including an undercover police officer, and gives Bill a cell phone with his father on the other end. Mr. Williamson tries to appeal to Bill, then reveals his mother died after a car accident, as a result of medication she had been taking for depression following Bill's first killing spree and disappearance. At that moment, Bill becomes suspicious of the undercover officer and kills him, then abruptly ends the conversation with his father. (Wikipedia, 2016).

Bill had no girl friend and no attachments, his mother had died (although he was able to sneak into the hospital and give her some flowers) and he really didn't give a damn about much more than killing as many people as he could. His father's appeals fell on deaf ears.

Moving on:

> Using hidden security cameras he implanted earlier, he notices SWAT teams converging on the basement and remotely detonates explosives, killing or incapacitating the officers. At Chip's urging, Bill commences with the live interview, during which he becomes

more specific about his rants in the disc and also espouses his opinions about killing innocent people. Asked if he regrets not being there when his mother died, he gets visibly upset but replies that his aim is bigger than family, and that it is about the survival of humanity. He then reveals his intention to die along with Chip before shooting him in the arm and releasing the other hostages.(Wikipedia, 2016).

Bill dismisses all the people in the television station basement – except for Chip. In fact, if there is any lack of realism in this movie it is the "bravado" that Chip showed, by way of his questions and comments to the armed Bill, that were out of whack. That white boy would not have had the guts to talk to an armed terrorist in that manner, and you can see their true gutlessness everywhere. This is a country that prides itself on spies, snipers and snitches. All that bravado stuff you see on television is what white folks WISH they could be. This movie makes great points and is well thought out in terms of revolutionary and guerilla approaches, but when it comes to the "stand tall" television man, reality was truly skewed.

He wounds Chip and then lets everyone else go:

> Bill immediately engages a SWAT team in a shootout before fleeing into the building's ventilation system, leaving behind a gas bomb. Just as the SWAT team discovers the bomb, it detonates, destroying the entire station and killing everyone inside, including Chip and the officers. Bill is then shown to be alive and well, watching a report of the station's destruction on his phone. As he does this, he spots a young girl reading a book and criticizes her for reading one. Bill then gives her a pistol and instructs her to use it to kill her parents and then herself before sending her off with a look of satisfaction on his face (Wikipedia, 2016).

As Chip says during one of his televised statements, "People die – and life goes on." He looks into the camera and says, "Too many people sucking up oru resources. Let's kill them. Let's just clean the world so the rest of us can sustain a little bit of life." He continues: "The United States government is funded by the rich. It keeps people on the level of children. They create illusions that everything is possible. WE live in a mind control dictatorship … It's a control mechanism for the rich. We lick the asses of Arabs … who come into our country."

He then finishes Chip off. He's ready to take a stand: "Let's do this the old fashioned Alamao way," he says. So WK7 Television is then blown up. The cops come in and sort through the rubble and believe that Bill must have died in the explosion. In the meantime Bill is chilling in a chair when a little girl walks by. He tells her to stop reading books and then hands her a pistol. "Go home and use it on your parents ," he says. The little girl walks off with the gun in tow. The movie ends with Bill staring into the camera: "I need you. I thank you for your help."

And this is what makes this move revolutionary. Not only did Bill accomplish his task, but he recruited and left a message for future revolutionaries to learn from and utilize.

Rampage: President Down (2016)

He started off by killing over a hundred in his small town, killed a hundred more in the second installment and now, while still in Washington, DC, Bill decides he's going to assassinate the president -- and he does just that. He is also able to kill other executives and achieves the global chaos that he was originally seeking.

Bill's scope is gradually grown larger. He begins by killing hundreds in his small hometown, goes to Washington, DC and destroys a TV station, some staff members and the news anchor. Now he is about to have an international impact, which is his goal. He wants everyone to pick up a gun and take to the streets and kill the rich. This, to me, would be a *real* revolution.

As Wikipedia informs us in a lengthy description:

> Three years after his second killing spree at a TV station in Washington D.C. (following which he was presumed dead in a massive explosion), Bill Williamson returns from hiding and, using a sniper rifle, assassinates the President of the United States, as well as the Vice-President and the Secretary of Defense. He then taunts the authorities, preparing for a final assault in which he expects to die as a martyr of his own cause, further establishing his iconic legacy and prompting thousands of people all across the USA to finally act upon their anger towards the elite and wealthy people, as instructed in Bill's former video statements, resulting in global chaos.(Wikipedia, 2016).

This is revolutionary thinking and strategizing. It may appear frightful to people who don't understand what revolution is, and that is because Americans have been "softened" by the overuse of the term by charlatans like Bernie Sanders, advertisers and these fake-ass macho movies that show the white man overcoming his oppressors with the greatest of ease.

This movie is mostly a dialogue on the global domination of America and how wrong the country has been since its inception. Williamson is hunted, hunkered down in a comfortable hole in the ground in the mountains. He has somehow arranged to have his woman and child come in to visit but toward the end of the movie he tells them they have to leave because the end, which he has prepared for, is near. As they leave he prepares for the final confrontation with the system's military minions.

Two FBI agents in particular - James Molokai and Vincent Jones -- have a hard on for Williamson. They have been making bold statements about him, all of which he has heard since he has their headquarters bugged, and in turn he has let them know that he knows about their personal lives, families, where their children attend school and so on. This only serves to incense them even more.

The movie is an incredible revolutionary statement about America's role in world domination and the right of the people to rebel against tyranny. As the military closes in the area outside of Williamson's hideout is incredibly well booby-trapped. He has land mines and several military-type machine guns on turrets that can be steered by remote control. He picks of scores of soldiers as they foolishly walk into death's jaws. With snow all around them, they are stepping on land mines and Williamson just sits and watches from his outside perch. As they get closer he makes a run for it but is finally cornered by Molokai and Jones.

He manages to kill one of the agents but is critically wounded by an barrage of bullets. As nightfall comes, he is sitting against a tree when Molokai walks upon him. He calls in the fact that he's "caught" Williamson, but before he can place him under arrest, Williamson dies.

The movie's ending is akin to the anticipation-oriented ending of "The Spook Who Sat by the Door" where the black revolutionaries are taking over even as their leader, Freeman, is slowly dying away. In "Rampage: President Down," Williamson may be dead but his wife is fully aware of her responsibilities. She calls the sitter for the child and once that is taken care of she gets prepared to go out and continue the work started by her beloved Williamson.

• *Triple 9*: **Terrorism and Counter-Terrorism**

Released in February of 2016, the movie "Triple 9" contributes to the revolutionary theme of this book because it prepares those who want to overthrow the system with a very realistic scenario of what the police state will do in their counter-terrorism efforts.

Don't let the generic snippets of the movie's plot fool you; this movie is a realistic portrayal of cops as they really are, the types of moves that SWAT-type police groups make, and the strategy and tactics used by those who want to commit a crime and know how to enlist the help of the police in order to do so.

According to once movie review source, Rotten Tomatoes (2016),

> In TRIPLE NINE, a crew of dirty cops is blackmailed by the
> Russian mob to execute a virtually impossible heist and the only

way to pull it off is to manufacture a 999, police code for "officer down." Their plan is turned upside down when the unsuspecting rookie they set up to die foils the attack, triggering a breakneck action-packed finale tangled with double-crosses, greed and revenge.

They were not just dirty cops; they were dirty cops who knew what they were doing and wanted to get paid. The only problem is when a group of two (dyad) becomes a group of three (triad), power shifts begin to take place. Marcus (Anthony Mackie) and his partner, another cop named Jorge (Clifton Collins, Jr.) had it all planned in cahoots with non-cop Michael Atwood (played by Chiwetel Ejiofor) is is a flunky for the Russian Jewish Mafia until Marcus gets a new partner, a street-wise white boy named Chris Allen (Casey Affleck) who plays by the book and has no idea that Marcus and the others are planning a major heist.

And here's where the link to "revolution" comes in: they want to pull what is called a "Triple 9." Triple 9 is code for "officer down." They are going to set up a fellow cop and have the police in Atlanta all swarm on one side of the projects while they commit a robbery nearby.

Reviewer Justin Chang (2016) had this to say:

> A crew of dirty cops is blackmailed by the Russian mob to execute a virtually impossible heist. The only way to pull it off is to manufacture a 999, police code for "officer down". Their plan is turned upside down when the unsuspecting rookie they set up to die foils the attack, triggering a breakneck, action-packed finale filled with double-crosses, greed and revenge

The issue that makes this movie "revolutionary" in my book is the planning that went into the goal to steal money. These cops knew that if they called in the numbers "999", which meant "officer down," all the cops would immediately flood the area. And if they did that, this would dievert the attention of the cops and therefore clear the area that the group wanted to rob. This is a revolutionary act: going against the system. And as one of the group's members, Jorge Rodriguez (played by Clifton Collns, Jr.) said, "I ain't afraid of taking out no cops." This is another revolutionary statement.

IS REVOLUTION POSSIBLE? INEVITABLE?

Those of you reading this book are probably believing that revolution in America is not possible and that if we engage white folks, we would lose. But there are two things that I know, for a fact: (1) race relations in this country are not going to get any better. Even with the spate of interracial marriages and mulatto kids running around, white supremacy is always going to serve as the foundation for this nation's political, economic, social and philosophical views and values and (2) white folks would rather destroy this country before turning it over to people of color. If you understand these two basic points of fact, then you need know little else. Under such conditions, revolution is not also possible and inevitable, but in my view, preferable when you consider what will happen – what IS happening – if we sit back and do nothing.

Here are some facts for your consideration.

Milton White, a brother who would serve as the director of the Black Studies Department here at UNO for a short time, and who worked with Senator Chambers and other brothers to organize patrols that followed the cops and a group called "The People's Regent," had a long history of involvement in the black struggle. White who spent most of is adult life in the U.S. Air Force, parted company with it after he and Sgt. Maynard Jordan III established the Malcolm X Association at Vandenberg Air Force Base, Calif., to express educational and cultural self-determination of the black military.

In November of 1970, White wrote an article for The Black Scholar titled, "Self-Determination for Black Soldiers." But here is the most telling part of the article, most germane to the inevitability of revolution in America:

> … The likelihood of Armed Forces being used gains black people in simple urban unrest, is very grate indeed. Already we have the example of the 4,000 paratroopers and Marines put on standby by Defense secretary Melvin R. Laird and Attorney General John Mitchell to reinforce the police and National Guard in New Haven this May during the popular rally preceding the trial of Bobby Seale. As far as armed revolution is concerned there is no question but the government would move swiftly and ruthlessly to annihilate fighters and to relocate other aroused blacks for the duration of the emergency. If the level of consciousness is high, and there is every indication that it would have been to trigger the ultimate conflict, this could mean years of concentration camps, followed by a long period of rehabilitation and finally apartheid (p. 41).

Then, there's the well-known issue of the concentration camps. Ever heard of the King Alfred Plan? The brothers and the sisters in the movement have. And it ain't no joke. Here's a primer for those of you who spend more time scratching your ass than you do reading a book:

> … In the event of widespread and continuing and coordinated racial disturbance in the United States, King Alfred at the discretion of the President is to be put into action immediately.

> Participating Federal Agencies: National Security Council,
> Department of Justice *849-899, Central Intelligence Agency,
> Federal Bureau of Investigation, Defense Department ... Racial
> war must be considered inevitable. When this emergency comes,
> expect the total involvement of all 22 million members of the
> minority ... Once this project is launched its goal is to terminate
> once and for all the threat to the whole of American society ..."
> King Alfred is reinforced by the Internal Security Act of 1950
> (McCarran Act) which provides for detention of persons who can
> "reasonably" be expected to participate in acts of sabotage or
> espionage (White, 1970: 41).

Dr. Milton White was one of the many good brothers who came through Omaha, made their contributions and then went on about his business after being ostracized by the white community in Omaha, in his case the administration of the University of Nebraska at Omaha.

One thing is for sure: ***we Black folks in America are the vanguard for the world.*** I have always said that we are Africans genetically, but have just enough of the white man's savagery coursing through our veins to make formidable foes. Look at how many of our own people we have killed over the years over dice games, alcohol, members of the opposite sex. That attitude has to be harnessed and re-directed to the number one pain in the ass that we collectively have. And you know who that is.

A true revolutionary brother named James Forman, the author of "The Black Manifesto," taught long ago that black liberation struggle is not about separatism or militant integrationism via class struggle (a position taken by former so-called radical brothers to justify chasing white bitches). Black liberation is about liberating,

> ... all the people in the US and we will be instrumental in the
> liberation of colored people the world around ... We say that
> there must be a revolutionary black vanguard and that white
> people in this country must be willing to accept black leadership,
> for that is the only protection that black people have to protect
> ourselves from racism rising again in this country (Forman,
> 1970: 38-39).

Look at the African continent: full of brothers and sisters and what are they doing? Afraid to attack the white man while more than willing to stage coups and attack one another (e.g., Sudan, Nigeria, Somalia, Rwanda). We, the hybrids here in America are Africans in America, nothing less. And we have the warrior spirit and live in the heart of the American octopus. We can no longer leave world liberation to those who are its tentacle-gripped victims.

ASSATA SHAKUR: THERE MAY BE HOPE:

> "Now is the time for us to come together with one another, to
> organize, to speak out and speak up on behalf of each other.
> There is no time to waste, while we debate, define, and discuss;
> the enemy continues his genocidal plan. We need to bear in mind
> the Ashanti proverb: 'Two men in a burning house must not stop
> to argue.' "
>
> - Dr. Mutulu Shakur

All over the world there are black people who love this country, but hate what it stands for and despise the people running it. In all their arrogance and pomp, these white folks can't seem to understand this most obvious of facts. They truly think that they have the right to police the world, to rape it of its natural and human resources, and dominate small nations. The incidents on September 11th, 2001 were not "terrorist attacks;" it was payback from the orphans of the people that America has murdered in years past.

American creates revolutionaries with its racist and capitalist activity. They talk of a "global village" and now they want to control it. White folks cannot seem to live in harmony with any other people unless they are in charge. And there are some of us who just can't live with that arrangement.

As a case in point, I received from a brother named David X, the following statement. He says it is from the great Assata Shakur, a real sister from back in the day. But her fire still lives on. Titled, "To My People," following is the full text of that essay. All punctuation is original:

> To My People
> By Assata Shakur
>
> Black brothers, Black sisters, i want you to know that i love you
> and i hope that somewhere in your hearts you have love for me.
> My name is Assata Shakur (slave name joanne chesimard), and i
> am a revolutionary. A Black revolutionary. By that i mean that i
> have declared war on all forces that have raped our women,
> castrated our men, and kept our babies empty-bellied.
>
> I have declared war on the rich who prosper on our poverty, the
> politicians who lie to us with smiling faces, and all the mindless,
> heart-less robots who protect them and their property.

I am a Black revolutionary, and, as such, i am a victim of all the wrath, hatred, and slander that amerika is capable of. Like all other Black revolutionaries, amerikkka is trying to lynch me.

I am a Black revolutionary woman, and because of this i have been charged with and accused of every alleged crime in which a woman was believed to have participated. The alleged crimes in which only men were
supposedly involved, i have been accused of planning. They have plastered pictures alleged to be me in post offices, airports, hotels, police cars, subways, banks, television, and newspapers. They have offered over
fifty thousand dollars in rewards for my capture and they have issued orders to shoot on sight and shoot to kill.

I am a Black revolutionary, and, by definition, that makes me a part of the Black Liberation Army. The pigs have used their newspapers and TVs to paint the Black Liberation Army as vicious, brutal, mad-dog criminals. They have called us gangsters and gun molls and have compared us to such characters as john dillinger and ma barker. It should be clear, it must be clear to anyone who can think, see, or hear, that we are the victims. The victims and not the criminals.

It should also be clear to us by now who the real criminals are. Nixon and his crime partners have murdered hundreds of Third World brothers and sisters in Vietnam, Cambodia, Mozambique, Angola, and South Africa. As was proved by Watergate, the top law enforcement officials in this country are a lying bunch of criminals. The president, two attorney generals, the head of the fbi, the head of the cia, and half the white house staff have been implicated in the Watergate crimes.

They call us murderers, but we did not murder over two hundred fifty unarmed Black men, women, and children, or wound thousands of others in the riots they provoked during the sixties. The rulers of this country have always considered their property more important than our lives.
They call us murderers, but we were not responsible for the twenty-eight brother inmates and nine hostages murdered at attica. They call us murderers, but we did not murder and wound over thirty unarmed Black students at Jackson State—or Southern State, either.

They call us murderers, but we did not murder Martin Luther King, Jr., Emmett Till, Medgar Evers, Malcolm X, George

Jackson, Nat Turner, James Chaney, and countless others. We
did not murder, by shooting in the
back, sixteen-year-old Rita Lloyd, eleven-year-old Rickie
Bodden, or ten-year-old Clifford Glover. They call us murderers,
but we do not control or enforce a system of racism and
oppression that systematically murders Black and Third World
people. Although Black people supposedly comprise about
fifteen percent of the total amerikkkan population, at least sixty
percent of murder victims are Black. For every pig that is killed
in the so-called line of duty, there are at least fifty Black people
murdered by the police.

Black life expectancy is much lower than white and they do their
best to kill us before we are even born. We are burned alive in
fire-trap tenements. Our brothers and sisters OD daily from
heroin and methadone. Our babies die from lead poisoning.
Millions of Black people have died as a result of indecent
medical care. This is murder. But they have got the gall to call us
murderers.

They call us kidnappers, yet Brother Clark Squires (who is
accused, along with me, of murdering a new jersey state trooper)
was kidnapped on April z, 1969, from our Black community and
held on one million dollars' ransom in the New York Panther 21
conspiracy case. He was acquitted on May 13, 1971, along with
all the others, of 156 counts of conspiracy by a jury that took less
than two hours to deliberate. Brother Squires was innocent. Yet
he was kidnapped from his community and family. Over two
years of his life was stolen, but they call us kidnappers. We did
not kidnap the thousands of Brothers and Sisters held captive in
amerika's concentration camps. Ninety percent of the prison
population in this country are Black and Third World people who
can afford neither bail nor
lawyers.

They call us thieves and bandits. They say we steal. But it was
not we who stole millions of Black people from the continent of
Africa. We were robbed of our language, of our Gods, of our
culture, of our human dignity, of our labor, and of our lives.
They call us thieves, yet it is
not we who rip off billions of dollars every year through tax
evasions, illegal price fixing, embezzlement, consumer fraud,
bribes, kickbacks, and swindles. They call us bandits, yet every
time most Black people pick
up our paychecks we are being robbed. Every time we walk into
a store in our neighborhood we are being held up. And every

time we pay our rent the landlord sticks a gun into our ribs.

They call us thieves, but we did not rob and murder millions of Indians by ripping off their homeland, then call ourselves pioneers. They call us bandits, but it is not we who are robbing Africa, Asia, and Latin America of their natural resources and freedom while the people who live there are sick and starving. The rulers of this country and their flunkies have committed some of the most brutal, vicious crimes in history. They are the bandits. They are the murderers. And they should be treated as such. These maniacs are not fit to judge me, Clark, or any other Black person on trial in amerikkka. Black people should and, inevitably, must determine our destinies.

Every revolution in history has been accomplished by actions, although words are necessary. We must create shields that protect us and spears that penetrate our enemies. Black people must learn how to struggle by
struggling. We must learn by our mistakes.

I want to apologize to you, my Black brothers and sisters, for being on the new jersey turnpike. I should have known better. The turnpike is a checkpoint where Black people are stopped, searched, harassed, and assaulted. Revolutionaries must never be in too much of a hurry or make careless decisions. He who runs when the sun is sleeping will stumble many times.

Every time a Black Freedom Fighter is murdered or captured, the pigs try to create the impression that they have quashed the movement, destroyed our forces, and put down the Black Revolution. The pigs also try to
give the impression that five or ten guerrillas are responsible for every revolutionary action carried out in amerika. That is nonsense. That is absurd. Black revolutionaries do not drop from the moon. We are
created by our conditions. Shaped by our oppression. We are being manufactured in droves in the ghetto streets, places like attica, san quentin, bedford hills, leavenworth, and sing sing. They are turning out thousands of us. Many jobless Black veterans and welfare mothers are joining our ranks. Brothers and sisters from all walks of life, who are tired of suffering passively, make up the BLA.

There is, and always will be, until every Black man, woman, and child is free, a Black Liberation Army. The main function of the Black

Liberation Army at this time is to create good examples, to
struggle for Black freedom, and to prepare for the future. We
must defend ourselves and let no one disrespect us. We must
gain our liberation by any
means necessary.

It is our duty to fight for our freedom.
It is our duty to win.
We must love each other and support each other.
We have nothing to lose but our chains.

UHURU!

AFTERWORD: OUR REVOLUTIONARY GREATNESS

Power concedes nothing without a demand. It never did and it
never will. Find out just what people will submit to and you have
found out the exact amount of injustice and wrong which will be
imposed upon them and these will continue till they have resisted
either with words or blows or with both. The limits of tyrants are
prescribed by the endurance of those whom they suppress.
--Frederick Douglass (1849)

All Afro-Americans must begin to think like guerilla fighters,
since we are all "blood brothers" in the struggle. Let us learn
from our mistakes in the past. Appealing to a power structure
does no good. The only thing that power reacts to is more power.
If we don't think we can win, then there is no use in trying.
Cowards give up when the odds look bad. A guerilla fighter
knows he or she is right and attempts to win no matter what the
odds are
-- Max Stanford (1970)

The fact of the matter is, it was black pride, courage, activity and audacity that inspired the book, ***The Spook Who Sat By the Door.*** The movie came about seven years after the book was written. But the ideas passed on by author Sam Greenlee were no fantasy – street warfare actually took place, with much of it being suppressed by the white media (as the so-called "slave revolts" were back in the 1800s). And we are coming to that point in today's America.

In regard to the revolts of the 1960s, one scholar and revolutionary leader from the '60s provided some context:

> For a period of three hundred years, the United States was the
> scene of constant revolt. During this period, white Americans –
> especially in the South – developed a fear of the "black hordes"
> … Contrary to the oppressor's statistics, the slave revolts were
> well organized, involved thousands of slaves, and sometimes had
> international implications. These revolts occurred on the average
> of every three weeks for a three hundred year period … With the
> population of African captives in the United States much greater
> than "Charlie" has ever been willing to admit, with Americans
> were faced with a black takeover or black revolution. Black
> revolution plagued them constantly. There was never any peace
> of mind …. (p. 36).

And for the most part, this perception about black people, this fear of us "revolting" has always been at the back of the white man's mind. For this reason, he acts the way he does in Congress and develops policies to weaken us in various ways: welfare policy to foster dependency, tokenism to pit us against one another, various plots and ploys to get in and out of our communities without suspicion and so on. Even more than sex, I am willing to bet that the white man's number one fixation, especially since the 1960s, has always revolved around the question, "What we gonna do with these niggas?"

We have always fought. Following are a few examples of the "revolutionary spirit" of black people, here and elsewhere.

The Mau Mau rebellion gave the British oppressors of Kenya fits. From 1952 to 1959, the Mau Mau showed how they sickened of being controlled by colonial oppressors by the use of force. It started off as the Land Freedom Army, organized by the Kikuyu tribe, but then became something much more. Most of the LFA swore an oath: "We used to drink the oath. We swore we would not let white men rule us forever. We would fight them even down to our last man, so that man could live in freedom" said Jacob Njangi, an LFA fighter (Slaughter, 1999).

Earlier I talked of the white man's fear of "black hordes," remember? That is a universal fear. In the case of the LFA/Mau Mau, check out the following facts:

> Ten days into the start of emergency rule, almost 4,000 Africans
> had been arrested, but the attacks from the LFA continued. A
> wave of hysteria swept through the European settlers. In January
> 1953, after the killing of a European farmer and his family, angry
> settlers stormed government house demanding stronger action. In
> fact, ***more white settlers died in road accidents on the streets of
> Nairobi during the emergency than at the hands of the LFA***
> (Slaughter, 1999).

In response, the issue of the concentration/detention camps that comes up in the movie, becomes reality as the fearful British used brutality in an attempt to squash the rebellion. Take note:

> In late 1953 the British opened a new campaign, code named Operation Anvil, to cut off the supply network to the LFA ... On 24 April 1954, the police rounded up all the African inhabitants in the city – around 100,000 people. The 70,000 Kikuyu were separated and screened. Of them, up to 30,000 men were taken into holding camps. The families of the arrested men were pushed into the already overcrowded native reserves. In the rural areas Kikuyu were forced into fortified villages, where they lived under 23-hour curfew. This policy, known as "villagisation," was claimed to be "purely protected and beneficial for the Africans." It gave the colonial authorities total control over the Kikuyu (Slaughter, 1999).

Sound familiar? The Mau Mau never gave up, and in 1960 the state of emergency was lifted. A year later, Jomo Kenyatta was freed form jail and in 1963, Kenya was granted independence. Fight to the last man and never give up. That is the revolutionary's credo.

Back to the states, a similar philosophy was a part of Nat Turner's 1831 rebellion during slavery. As Stanford reminds us,

> Nat Turner's philosophy of "strike by night and spare none" is very important because it shows us that Turner knew the psychology of white America, and that we had leadership with the guerilla instinct. Turner knew what black terrorism meant t the whites, and struck, even though the odds were against him (p. 37).

Nat Turner and his band of men were bent on killing every white person they came across. They didn't even spare the children since Nat ordered, "nits make lice." Before they were finished they had killed 57 white folks and sent a panic across the white community that had many of them locking themselves in the houses and praying for help. The militia finally caught up with the freedom fighters and the day they lynched Nat, it rained and thundered – a sign from above that Nat had predicted would take place. This scared white folks even more.

The fact is, there were more than 1,500 recorded "slave insurrections" against the white man. This means that there must have been three or four times that many. The media then, as now, does not want to frighten its white readership – so they suppress reality for the benefit of the very cowards who try to pawn themselves off as saviors. The white man's fear of "black hordes" became evident with the passage of the Fugitive Slaves Law of 1850.

A brother who few of today's black folks remember is Robert F. Williams. Long before he wrote the book *Negroes With Guns,* however, it was Williams who should be credited with advancing the theory of "urban guerilla warfare." From 1957 to 1961, Williams and his group defended the community – armed to the teeth.

Williams spearheaded a movement to defend the black community of Monroe, Louisiana and the Klan and any other crackers that might want to ride down on black homes, the way they did in the movie, "Rosewood." Williams was a real warrior, and didn't play around, as Harkness (1996) makes clear:

> Williams was born in 1925, but as a young man moved to
> Detroit, where he worked at a Ford auto plant. Williams found
> himself in the middle of the Detroit race riot in 1943 and had to
> defend himself and others from racist white mobs. Later he
> joined the U.S. Marines. Upon his discharge, he worked in New
> Jersey and then decided to return to his southern hometown to
> take up the right against Jim Crow segregation and the Ku Klux
> Klan. Williams organized a large chapter of the NAACP made
> up of working-class Blacks from Monroe. He also organized a
> chapter of the National Rifle Association that defended the Black
> community against racist assault.

In most black folks' life there is a "straw" that breaks the camels back, that last insult that should make most of us aware of the fact that we are at war. Most of our people suppress their anger and go on about their usual ways, pretending that race relations are getting better and cowering at the thought of fighting back against racist oppression. For Williams and other brothers and sister in Monroe, Louisiana, that straw was a case that people call the "Kissing Case:"

> Two Black boys, ages seven and nine, were charged with
> "assaulting and molesting a white female" after the older one had
> been kissed by a seven-year-old white girl. They were arrested,
> thrown into the county jail, and then sentenced by a judge to the
> State Reformatory for Negro Boys until they were 21. The judge
> explained when the seven-year-old boy witnessed the kiss it had
> caused "his morals to become seriously impaired and he needed
> a term for indefinite rehabilitation" (Harkness, 1996).

From there, Williams and others organized the Committee to Combat Racial Injustice, which publicized this incident all over the world. The boys were finally let go after four months. But Williams did more than organize protests.

Williams' rifle club did not play around. When Klansman threatened to ride down on the home of a black doctor, Williams and the boys built some sandbag fortifications and waited for them. When those racists arrived, Williams and company opened fire, and those crackers split. Shortly after that the city passed an ordinance against KKK motorcades, which previously had been escorted by the local police!

Because he was such a threat, he and his family got set up by the FBI on bogus kidnapping charges and the Williams' fled to Cub. But a real revolutionary never rests, and when he got there he broadcast a radio show called "Radio Free Dixie," back into the United States (Harkness, 1996).

We've always had warriors who were willing to go toe-to-toe with the oppressor. And the white man knows this, which is why he spends so much time attempting to "define" our leadership for us.

On into the 1960s and early 1970s, black people had it going on. We stood toe-to-toe with the most powerful military in the history of the world and kicked their ass. They came at us and we burned their cities. They shot down our people, and we turned out their streets. We forced them to come to the table and when they came, we forgot who in the hell we were. These Uncle Tom leaders who claimed to speak for us sold us down the river: Bayard Rustin, Martin Luther King, Jr., Floyd McKissick, A. Philip Randolph, Whitney Young and the rest. By the time those white boys got finished with these coons, we had let them (the white folks) up off their knees, settled for some half-assed Federal jobs, and enabled them to buy time to plan our next setback.

As unorganized as they ended up being, we cannot forget the Black Panther Party for Self-Defense. I lived near Oakland during the time and we read about and watched on TV as those brothers stood down the cops at every turn. Every now and then there would be a shootout, but most of those were "Custer Stands" against huge numbers of cops, which ended in murder of those brothers. Black men and women dropped out of college to join the Panthers, and young children adored them. White folks in California had to pass the Mumford Gun Bill to stop people from brandishing weapons openly, because the Panthers were doing that all up and down the streets of Oakland, challenging and following cops, and making sure that "power to the people" was much more than just a catchy slogan. It was a great time.

Other groups came along with a similar philosophy: the Latinos had the Brown Beret, the Chinese had The Red Guard, and the Natives had the American Indian Movement behind Dennis Banks and Russell Means. White boy revolutionaries (the Weathermen, mainly), who didn't play around, were blowing shit up on the east coast. Open warfare was a threat and the oppressor was afraid.

We opened up people's eyes to racism and some capitalized on it on the big screen. Like the groups that scared whitey, many of the movies that dealt with racism head on "mysteriously" disappeared or were not given their due. Before the Spook Who Sat By the Door, there were other flicks.

We talk about "To Kill a Mockingbird" or "The Learning Tree," but people forget the fact that in 1970 there was a movie called, "The McMasters," where Brock Peters was married to an Indian woman played by Nancy Kwan. He had returned from the war and moved back onto the land of his former master, played by Burl Ives. But he's quick to find out that he is "free" in name only. The only people who would help him farm it were Native Americans, but white boys got jealous and continued to harass both Peters and Kwan. The movie was so controversial there were two endings: in one, racism wins and in the other one, racism is overcome. You can guess which one is most popular with white folks.

In 1972, a year before "The Spook Who Sat By The Door" shocked white America, there was another movie that had a similar impact: it was called "The Man," and it starred James Earl Jones. While the movie was bullshit for the most part, one scene where a militant reporter fires a barrage of questions at the black man who becomes president makes points most similar to those made in Spook.

And, of course, there was the written word of revolution by some of our best and brightest.

In November of 1970, a new publication swept America with the best in black nationalist thought. It was called ***The Black Scholar***, and in November of 1970, it carried a theme, "The Black Soldier." One of the articles in that publication was written by Max Stanford, who was then the national field chairman of the Revolutionary Action Movement (RAM). The article that he wrote for that publication, which will quoted from in this paper, was titled, "Black Guerilla Warfare: Strategy and Tactics." I quote freely from it in this brief book because it was a precursor for much of what was discussed in the movie, and most of what was in this article can still be applied today.

The thing that ***Spook*** had that others lacked was the fact that black people are scene out-thinking, out-planning and out-fighting white folks. While the black movies of the 1970s (judgmentally and incorrectly dubbed "blaxploitation flicks") would show blacks physically defeating white folks, much of it was haphazard and institutions remained intact. Not so for ***The Spook Who Sat By The Door.***

A brother named Colin Ferguson was immediately dubbed "insane" when, on December 7, 1993, he got on a Long Island Rail Road train and shot down 25 people, killing six white folks. It was found that he planned the shootings in advance as a reaction to a number of incidents where white folks had disrespected him. Ferguson rightly claimed that people and institutions were against him. What he said was that WHITE folks were out to get him and in fact, in court made it a matter of public record that although the shootings involved people from other races, his main concern or target was "white people." And the only reason he wanted suburban Nassau County to be the "venue" for his actions was because he didn't want to embarrass African-American New York City mayor David Dinkins. What is insane about THIS? Ferguson was convicted on February 17, 1995 for murder and got a life sentence – 200 years in prison -- for the crimes.

Revolts, riots and relevant response. This is what our people have stood for in the racial battle that has been brewing ever since our arrival on these shores. Today's generations may not appreciate what we have gone through in the quest for liberation, but I certainly do.

I believe that the thing that pissed white folks off more than seeing black people taking apart their military and their nation, is the thinking part: despite all their surveillance and treachery, they were duped. They were outsmarted by people who they believed were inferior to them. And the book was, in my view, a primer for how to overthrow America. The statistics cited in the movie (I address this later) were accurate for the time, the logistics of the inner city and the city blocks and rooftops remain the same to this day. If the book was a primer for revolution, then the film was an actual play-by-play game plan.

CONCLUSION

The movie, "The Spook Who Sat By The Door," was made public thirty-eight years ago. Not the syrupy contrived bullshit inherent in flicks like "Do the Right Thing," or "Tick, Tick, Tick." Not the "stop just short of protest" crap like, "A Time to Kill" or "Cornbread, Earl and Me." Not the "swallow the white man's warm spit" as depicted in "The Learning Tree," "Roots" and "Mississippi Burning."

Straight up revolution. And that's why it was banned.

Why did I write this book? Because I want to make a contribution to the struggle that must be. It is only a matter of time. As the old-timers say, "all the cotton's been picked, and all the shoes have been shined." We live in critical times when all around us we see people fighting the powers that be and we here in America sit in our living rooms, skinning and grinning, waiting for the white man's skewed newscasts to tell us more lies about what is going on.

When will you sicken of going to church on Sunday and having some coward tell you that the devil has a pitchfork and that hell is someplace you'll go when you die? When will you sicken of giving your money, "paying tithes" as you call it, while some former pimp or drug hustler who claims to have "been called" continues to bullshit and bamboozle you about your status here on earth?

When will the day come when you will see the foolishness inherent in marching and protesting the death of a slain black person by the police, instead of doing something about the police? When will you do to the white man what far too many of your more than willingly do to your spouses, your children or some other person with the same color skin as you?

These people are getting bolder. They steal our cultural nuances and pawn them off as our own. They take our greatest physical attributes and then find white folks who might have them and turn those white folks into "superstars." They impose their bullshit aesthetic on our women so much to the point where many of them are now walking around with horse hair on their heads. They mis-educate our children and then kick them out of school when the kids tell them to get fucked. We pray for a job in their system and then judge our friends and others by which one found the most powerful white man to employ them – in other words, "adopt" them.

White people, in general, hate black people, in general. That is what State Senator Ernie Chambers has correctly contended all these years and he's been proven right, all these years. This interracial dating and marriage bullshit is just a smokescreen to cover up the fact that the white man is tired of his woman. He's shown her he hates her all these years, but finally he's found someplace he can toss her – to men of color. He can create kids in his test tubes and by jacking off into a petrie dish. He's replaced her in the kitchen with the microwave oven, the dishwasher and the deluxe do-it-all ready-made food snacks.

The white man downsizing his family life because the only thing he wants is an offspring to carry on his tradition and legacy of oppression. He segregates himself from you and instead of turning your community's power inward, you beg to live next to him where you will be despised, harassed, dogged out and otherwise made to feel worse than you did before you moved there. What will it take, oh, sisters and brothers of the 21st century?

There may still be some hope. There are some good brothers and sisters left, but don't base it on the size of the city. My "theory of a thousand" says that no matter how big the urban area is, we only have about a thousand good brothers and sisters who are willing to throw down. That means that big cities like Chicago, Los Angeles, New York, Philly and so on have a whoooole bunch of Uncle Toms. Small cities like Omaha, Newark and Milwaukee, we have a lot of toms, but we have a good number of "down" black folks as well.

As for Hollywood, well did you know that Tim Reid ("Frank's Place," WKRP in Cincinnati") and his fine wife Daphne Maxwell Reid ("Fresh Prince of Bel-Air") played a major role in getting this movie re-done? The white boys tried to hide the movie by putting it under another title. Nobody could locate it until Tim and Daphne went about the arduous task of searching. When they finally found it, they didn't horde it or prostitute it as most people would have done. They purchased the movie under the fake title and then – returned it to its rightful owner, Sam Greenlee!

That act took courage and heart. But where are the Hollywood blacks who talk black all the time: the Blair Underwoods, Wesley Snipes' and Marla Gibbs' who have good hearts, but can't be found when a movie like this needs some support. I guess they say what most black people say when you ask them why they do nothing. Same answer: "gotta eat."

As Nathan Hare (1970) once wrote,

> It is not enough to clinch our fists, to wear militant garb, or generally to acquire the most menacing look; not enough to read black history, listen to jazz music, smoke pot, or write down pretty poetry, author weighty books or revolutionary songs. Instead, in the words of Frantz Fanon, we "Must fashion the revolution with the people. And if you fashion it with the people, the songs will come by themselves, and of themselves" (p. 3).

I have been involved with three race riots while in high school. Those whites I went to school with want to blame others, but I was on the front lines when I would see hundreds of them charging up the hill that divided the middle school (Riverview) from the high school where I was but a sophomore; I was there when my beautiful sister, Betty, had her head cut open by a pop bottle hurled by some cowardly cracker; and I was there when these white folks, who claimed to be our friends, were rocking the school bus we were on and indeed, went home (across the street) and dragged back their drunken, disorderly and club-toting older brothers and sisters. I stood strong, as anyone can tell you.

I have used four African-American newspapers, three of which I was founder and publisher of, three major university student newspapers, two radio talk shows, and two separate cable access television shows to express my commitment to the struggle, my disdain for the oppressor, and my love for black people (and other people of color). I have taken on corporations ranging from Mutual of Omaha, the University of Nebraska, the University of Wisconsin-Madison, Denney's, People's Express Airlines, to Federal Express, the Racine Journal-Times, the Bradley Foundation, the Omaha World Herald, and many others. And I have kicked their ass in defense of my people.

My brothers and sisters in Milwaukee, Dallas and Omaha, I have spent more than 40 years of my life preparing to deal with our situation. Whether on campus or in the streets of Pittsburg (CA.), Omaha (NE.), Lincoln (NE.), Chicago (IL.), Milwaukee (WI.) or Racine (WI.), I did all I could to establish a foundation for black pride and autonomy. I did all I could to expose and embarrass our oppressors, defend those of us who could not get help elsewhere, and show by example that I could and would not be broken. It has cost me dearly. And yet, the track record speaks for itself.

Therefore it pangs me deeply when I see that my beloved black people, my brothers and sisters, have learned so little, and that, for the most part, we continue to make the same mistakes we made in the 1920s and 30s.

Even as I write these words, ABC television is airing a story about the sterilization of "thousands of poor people" between the years 1929 and 1974, most of them black, many of them in North Carolina. These white people were sterilizing people of color, having developed a program that would prevent "undesirables" from reproducing. It was their belief that "these kind of people" were genetically predisposed to reproduce poorly therefore deserved to be sterilized – without their permission. In fact, most of the people sterilized were not even told.

According to the reporter, Keith Garvin, 33 states practiced sterilization at one time. In Windfall, North Carolina, a sister who was sterilized after giving birth to one child, has since graduated from college and her son is now an engineering consultant. While the news report focused on this woman, Elaine Riddick, the fact is, white folks did this. In all their arrogance, they believed they had the right to decide who's "defective" and who is not. It's called genetic engineering and they're still doing it.

The ten (10) movies about "revolution" that I have analyzed in this book all have a different orientation, but it is the fact that the target – white America – is in all of them that we should think about. Everybody was fighting, either to take or to protect; to defend or to develop. These are revolutionary intentions even when the end result may seem like a failure. To speak truth to power is the first step in the life of the revolutionary.

Those in power give us little choice in what we must do, because they never learn. Like the white kid in the schoolyard who gets his ass kicked for calling a black kid a "nigger," only to get back up and say it again, this white society just keeps up its racist ways, keeps coming up with one racist policy and procedure after another, one more segregated suburb after another, one more immigrant buffer zone after another. Mark my words, they will not be satisfied until there are more riots and more fires and more cities burning. This is the only thing that will get their attention.

Remember well the line from Freeman in, "The Spook Who Sat By the Door:" "In guerilla warfare, the winning is in not losing. When you sleep on the floor, you can't fall out of bed." The time has come to understand that we are dealing with a race of people who simply do not get it. ***But one day soon, they will.***

Trust me – they will. As the Last Poets once stated in their poem, "Chastisement":

No, that was not a riot/
That they saw down in the slums/
It was just a dress rehearsal/
For things that are yet to come …

REFERENCES

Chang, Justin (2016, February 17). Film review: 'Triple 9.' Retrieved from http://variety.com/2016/film/reviews/triple-9-review-casey-affleck-1201707725/

Dermer, Alexander (2012, August 10). Invasion USA: Film Review. Weekend notes. Retrieved from http://www.weekendnotes.com/invasion-usa-film-review/

Ebert, Roger. (1973, July 26). Badge 373. Retrieved from http://www.rogerebert.com/reviews/badge-373-1973

Ebert, Roger (1985, September 27). Invasion USA. Retrieved from http://www.rogerebert.com/reviews/invasion-usa-1985

Ebert, Roger (2012, November 20). Red Dawn. Retrieved from http://www.rogerebert.com/reviews/red-dawn-2012

Hare, Nathan. (1970, November). From the publisher. *The Black Scholar*.

Harkness, Holly. (1996, November). Robert F. Williams Memorial honors life of struggle. *The Militant,* 41, (18).

,Hood, Gregory. (2016). Red Dawn (1984). Retrieved from http://www.counter-currents.com/2012/12/red-dawn-1984/

Robey, Tim (2014, October 30). Invasion of the Body Snatchers (1956), review A powerful subtext illustrates the political paranoia of the McCarthy era, says Tim Robey. Retrieved from http://www.telegraph.co.uk/culture/film/filmreviews/11198302/invasion-of-the-body-snatchers-film-review-tim-robey.html

Rotten Tomatoes (2016). Triple 9. Retrieved from
https://www.rottentomatoes.com/m/triple_9/

Slaughter, Barbara. (1999, September 15). How Britain crushed the "Mau Mau
rebellion." *World Socialist Web.*

White, Milton. (1970, November). Self-determination for black soldiers. *The
Black Scholar.*

Williams, John A. (1968). *The Man Who Cried I Am.* New York: Signet Books.

Stanford, Max. (1970, November). Black guerilla warfare: Strategy and tactics.
The Black Scholar, 2, (3).

The Movie Bastard (2013, September 22). Retro review: Invasion USA. Retrieved
from https://moviebastards.com/2013/09/22/retro-review-invasion-usa/

Wikipedia (2016). Badge 373. Retrieved from
https://en.wikipedia.org/wiki/Badge_373

Wikipedia (2016). Rampage. Retrieved from
https://en.wikipedia.org/wiki/Rampage_(2009_film)

Wikipedia (2016). Rampage: Capital punishment. Retrieved from
https://en.wikipedia.org/wiki/Rampage:_Capital_Punishment

Wikipedia (2016). Rampage: President down. Retrieved from
http://www.bing.com/search?q=rampage%3A+president+down&src=IE-
TopResult&FORM=IETR02&conversationid=

Yette, Samuel F. (1971). *The Choice: The Issue of Black Survival in America.*
New York: G.P. Putnam.